# Teaching Gifted Kids in the Regular Classroom

### Strategies and Techniques
### Every Teacher Can Use
### to Meet the Academic Needs
### of the Gifted and Talented

Susan Winebrenner

Edited by Pamela Espeland

free spirit
PUBLiSHiNG®

Works
for kids™

# DEDICATION

To Joan Franklin Smutny, who made me believe I could be a real writer, and to my husband, Neil, who made the computer behave as it should for a real writer, thereby patiently calming my madness.

# ACKNOWLEDGMENTS

Many thanks to the people who believed before I did that I had important messages to bring to teachers:

Dr. Art Jones, Superintendent, for his mentorship of my transition from classroom teacher to teacher guide;

Jim Bellanca of the IRI Group for providing me with my first opportunities to actually teach in a continuing education setting;

Arlene Bloom for encouraging me to create new workshops on any topic I wished, and for giving unequivocal support of my work as a consultant;

Judy Galbraith for providing a positive role model for aspiring female writers;

Pat Butti, my friend and spiritual guide, who started me on this path by asking innocently, "Why not?"

Thanks to the teachers and administrators who have believed my messages enough to try out the strategies in their schools and give me lots of wonderful feedback about the successes they have enjoyed.

Thanks also to my editor, Pamela Espeland, for never losing sight of my vision about how I wanted this book to serve teachers.

Thanks finally to my parents, Sam and Lil Schuckit, for always believing that I could do whatever I set my mind to do, and for constantly communicating their support and pride in my ventures.

Winebrenner, Susan
Teaching gifted kids in the regular classroom : strategies and techniques every teacher can use to meet the academic needs of the gifted and talented / Susan Winebrenner : edited by Pamela Espeland.
   p.  cm.
   Includes bibliographical references and index.
   ISBN 0-915793-47-4
   1. Gifted children—Education—United States.
I. Espeland, Pamela, 1951– . II. Title.
LC3993.9.W56 1992
371.95'0973—dc20           92-20926
                         CIP

Cover and book design by MacLean and Tuminelly
20 19 18 17 16 15 14 13 12 11
Printed in the United States of America

FREE SPIRIT PUBLISHING INC.
400 First Avenue North, Suite 616 • Minneapolis, MN 55401
phone (612) 338-2068 • fax (612) 337-5050
help4kids@freespirit.com • www.freespirit.com

The excerpt from "The Memoirs of Jesse James" on page 2 is © 1970 by Richard Brautigan, reprinted by permission of The Helen Brann Agency, Inc.

The Compactor form introduced in Chapter 2 and used throughout this book is adapted from *The Schoolwide Enrichment Model: A Comprehensive Plan for Educational Excellence* by Joseph S. Renzulli and Sally Reis, Creative Learning Press, P.O. Box 320, Mansfield Center, CT 06250. Used with permission.

The Taxonomy of Thinking chart on page 68 and the Build Blocks to Think chart on page 80 are adapted from *Taxonomy of Educational Objectives: The Classification of Educational Goals: Handbook I: Cognitive Domain* by Benjamin S. Bloom et al. Copyright © 1956, 1984 by Longman Publishing Group. Reprinted with permission from Longman Publishing Group.

The concept for the Guidelines for Creating Student-Made Learning Centers on page 78 and the Examples of Student-Made Learning Centers on page 79 was developed and submitted by Dariel J. McGrath, Lansing, IL.

Super Sentence: Level One on page 102 and Super Sentence: Level Two on page 104 are adapted from *Super Sentences* by Susan Winebrenner. Mansfield Center, CT: Creative Learning Press, 1989. Used with permission.

# ★ CONTENTS ★

# ★ LIST OF REPRODUCIBLE FORMS ★

# ★ LIST OF FIGURES ★

# INTRODUCTION

Of all the students you are teaching in a given class, which group do you think will probably learn the *least* this year? It may surprise you to find that in a class that has a range of abilities (and which class doesn't?), it is the *most able,* rather than the least able, who will learn less new material than any other group.

How does this happen? Mostly, it's because of a phenomenon with which we are all too familiar: the scope-and-sequence monster. Each year, we are given a certain slice of a student's entire school curriculum to teach, and we feel intense pressure and responsibility to teach everything assigned to our grade or subject to all of our students. The problem comes when we accidentally confuse the meanings of two important words, *teach* and *learn*.

A teacher's responsibility is not to teach the *content*. A teacher's responsibility is to teach the *students*, and to make sure that all students learn new content every day. With gifted students, the reality is that they already know a significant amount of the curriculum we are planning to teach, and they can learn new material in much less time than their age peers.

Recently, a fourth-grade teacher who attended one of my two-day workshops had an interesting experience you may relate to. After the first day of the workshop, she started thinking about how happy she had felt the day before, when all of the students in her top reading group got "A"'s on the end-of-the-unit test. She now wondered whether their grades actually reflected what they had learned from her. Was it possible that they already knew the material before coming to her class?

Since there were two weeks between each workshop day, she decided to find the answer to her question. The next day, with no advance warning, she gave these same students the end-of-the-unit test for the following unit. They were tested on the skills and the vocabulary, but not on the content of the stories, which, of course, they had not yet read. Again, they got all "A"'s.

This experience was one of the most startling of the teacher's career. She began to consider alternate methods of teaching her best readers.

When gifted students discover that they already know a lot of what the teacher or book will be covering, they have little choice but to dutifully go through the assigned curriculum, waiting and hoping for the rare times when there will be something new or challenging for them to learn. Enabling you to make those times happen more frequently for your gifted students is what this book is all about.

Because of my own experience—first as a classroom teacher, and now as a teacher trainer—I can identify with and completely understand the terror that strikes most teachers as they contemplate what might result from finding out what their gifted students already know, giving them credit for it, and providing alternate activities. This terror has two names: one is "losing control," and the second is "what am I supposed to do with them when I find out they have already learned most of what I am planning to teach this year?"

I promise you that the management strategies described in this book will calm your fears. I promise you that they will work with your mixed-ability groups of students. I promise you that there will be no resentment on the part of the other students as they see the gifted students "doing their own thing." I promise you that you will not have to spend very much time preparing "extra" materials for the gifted students. Finally, I promise you the following results for your gifted students:

• They will be more highly motivated.

• They will be more productive—they will actually get their work done.

• They will have more positive feelings about school.

• Their parents will be very pleased with what's happening in your class.

• Their teacher (you) will be very pleased with their attitude and productivity and with the professionally satisfying results your efforts produce.

Furthermore, their teacher (you) will avoid the "Jesse James Syndrome." When asked what it was like to be gifted in a regular classroom, a gifted student adapted some words from Richard Brautigan's poem, "The Memoirs of Jesse James," to create a metaphor for his school experiences:

> *All the time I just sat there...waiting,*
> *Waiting for something new to learn.*
> *My teachers should have ridden with Jesse James*
> *For all the learning time*
>         *they have stolen from me!*

To make sure that your students never think this of you, simply use the strategies presented in this book. Watch what happens as gifted students become more motivated to work, less sullen and hostile, and more likely to enjoy school and your teaching. Watch how the other kids don't object when some of their classmates are engaged in alternate activities. Listen to what the parents of the gifted students say as they thank you for making their child's school experience so enjoyable and rewarding. Notice the positive feelings you experience as you realize you are truly meeting the special learning needs of your gifted students.

Each chapter presents a particular teaching/management strategy. Scenarios profile actual students* with whom the strategy has been used—either by me, or by a teacher I have trained—so you will be able to notice similar characteristics, needs, and responses in your students. The strategy itself is described in step-by-step detail. Frequently asked questions about the strategy are answered, and a summary reviews the main points.

Many strategies presented in this book make use of special forms. When these forms are generally useful, I have included reproducible versions for you to photocopy. I often customize basic forms to meet the needs of specific students. My customized forms are shown as examples; please feel free to revise them to fit your unique teaching style and your students' needs. Instructions and tips for using the forms are provided in the chapters.

The strategies in chapters 1–3 are designed to be used with subject areas that lend themselves to pretesting, because it is likely that some of your students will have retained prior learning. The strategies in chapters 4–6 are designed to be used with subject areas that appear to represent new learning for students, such as science, social studies, and interdisciplinary and/or thematic units.

Chapter 7 covers appropriate reading instruction for gifted students, and Chapter 8 discusses how to evaluate their work. Chapter 9 helps you to understand the special needs of gifted students in cooperative learning experiences, and Chapter 10 describes a method that allows a school to group gifted students together without necessarily grouping students of other ability levels.

Chapter 11 discusses miscellaneous issues, such as acceleration, how to locate appropriate teaching materials, and how to deal with parents, administrators, and colleagues. An Activities appendix at the end presents games, puzzles, and other challenges gifted kids love; I know, because

---

*The students are actual, but their names are fictional with one exception: James T. Myers, whose real name is used in his scenario in Chapter 2.

I have used them in my own classes. Finally, you'll find a list of companies that specialize in gifted education materials, along with addresses and telephone numbers.

This book is designed to help you meet the educational needs of the gifted kids in your classroom. (Actually, you'll find that the strategies and techniques presented here will benefit *all* of your students, not just your gifted students—more about that later.) However, it is certainly *not* meant to replace other gifted education opportunities available in your district, or to serve as a reason for eliminating such opportunities. Gifted kids are gifted 24 hours a day, not just during those times they spend in special classes or on special projects or activities. When other elements of gifted programs are combined with differentiation in the regular classroom, as described here, gifted kids can experience *consistent* opportunities to enjoy learning and to be as productive as possible.

With that in mind, enjoy this book. It's written for you to use simply, without much fuss. All methods have been field tested with many teachers like yourself who have found them to work very well. Many of these teachers have told me, "I wish I had known about these methods before now—I would have always used them." I hope you will feel the same.

Let's get started.

Susan Winebrenner

# THE GIFTED IDENTIFY THEMSELVES

If you feel unsure about how to identify the gifted students in your class, you're not alone. Many teachers share your uncertainty. You may have had little or no training in gifted education, because in most states, it has never been a required course in teacher education programs. Your administrators may know even less than you, since few of them have had training either. No wonder you worry about doing the right thing. What if you identify the wrong students, and they're not "truly gifted?" What if you fail to identify the "truly gifted?"

Relax! You don't have to identify anyone. All you have to do is set up some learning opportunities that gifted students will jump at, and a magical thing happens: The opportunities allow gifted students to identify themselves.* Furthermore, your other students won't resent the "privileges" some students are getting because all students in your class will have the same chances to qualify for those privileges. With these strategies, "equality" means equal opportunity for everyone.

## SCENARIO: AARON

Aaron was a fourth-grade boy with "great potential" who, according to most of his teachers, had made a career out of "wasting time and not working up to his ability." He had been denied permission to attend the gifted education class because of his poor work habits.

In my capacity as Coordinator of the Gifted Education Program, I offered to come into his class and demonstrate the "Most Difficult First" strategy, to see if it would help Aaron be more productive in math class and to convince his teacher to let him attend the gifted program meetings.

First, I taught a math lesson to the class. The concept was new, and I gave the students 20 minutes to begin their homework in class. When I wrote the assignment on the board, it looked like this:

Page 59, 11-25
☆ 21-25

Then I made the following announcement:

"Boys and girls, I have assigned 15 problems for your homework, because I think most of

---

*For a description of the characteristic behaviors of gifted and talented students, see Appendix A on pages 139-140.

you will need that much practice to master this lesson. However, I may be wrong. The problems become more difficult as the numbers get higher, and I have starred the five problems that represent the toughest problems on the page. Anyone in this class who can do the starred problems first—neatly, legibly, and with 80 percent accuracy—is done practicing. The problems must be completed and corrected before this math period is over."

Aaron had been in his characteristic "I-dare-you-to-make-me-work" slouch, with nothing on top of his desk, since he had stated he had no book or materials. As I finished my explanation, his head shot up, and we had the following conversation.

*AARON:* "Excuse me...what did you just say?"

*ME:* "What do you think I said?"

*AARON:* "I think you said that if I get those five problems right, and you can read them, I don't have to do my homework!"

*ME:* "That's correct."

*AARON:* "Uh, is my regular teacher going to do this tomorrow?"

*ME:* "I'm not sure, but I'll bet it has something to do with whether or not it works today."

*AARON:* "Yeah, right." (Pause.) "Uh, what happens if I get two wrong?"

*ME:* "Aaron, how much of the 20 minutes is left?"

*AARON:* "Oh, yeah. Right. Okay, I'll give it a try."

Aaron suddenly "found" his math book, a pencil, and some paper in his desk. He got right to work, finished the designated problems accurately and neatly, and was "done" with his homework. His teacher had the evidence she needed that he understood the concept, and Aaron had the joyful feeling that somehow he'd gotten away with something.

# STRATEGY:
## MOST DIFFICULT FIRST

When giving your class an assignment, start by determining which items represent the most difficult examples of the entire task. These might appear sequentially, near the end of the assignment,

or you might select them from various sections of the assignment. Five examples are a reasonable number, but you may choose a few more or less, depending on your judgment. Write the assignment on the board, star the Most Difficult First examples, then offer this explanation to the class:

"Boys and girls, the regular assignment should give just the right amount of practice for most of you to master the concept or skill. As a matter of fact, I expect most of you will need this much practice.

"However, some of you may have learned this material before and don't need as much practice this time. This opportunity is for you. Instead of doing the regular assignment, you may choose to do just the five starred problems. They are the most difficult problems in the assignment. When you finish, come to me and I'll check your work. The first person who gets all five correct will become the checker for the rest of the period.

"Once I announce who the checker is, anyone else who completes the five most difficult problems should stay at your desk, put your thumb up as a signal, and wait for the checker to get to you. If your paper meets the criteria, the checker will collect your paper to give to me.

"You may use any remaining time for anything you choose, as long as you meet two conditions: Don't bother anyone else, and don't call any attention to yourself. Anyone who can't meet these conditions will not be eligible tomorrow for this opportunity.

"During the practice time, I'll be helping students who are doing the regular assignment. If you think you will need help, you should start at the beginning of the assignment, since you obviously need more practice."

The reason this strategy works is very simple. Gifted students can learn even new concepts more quickly than their age peers, and they remember most of what they learn forever. So even if today's assignment represents new material to your grade level, your gifted math students can master the concept with much less practice than your average math students. That's part of what makes them gifted!

Most Difficult First allows gifted students to demonstrate their capability in 10-20 minutes, instead of the longer time many assignments require. It is advisable to allow students to qualify even if they make one error. In this way, you avoid causing anxiety for perfectionists, and you demonstrate that it's okay to make mistakes. However, the checker's paper must have all problems correct.

If you use the beginning of the next math period to check papers, the students who qualify may again have some free time. That's fine, as long as they keep doing whatever they choose without bothering anyone or calling attention to themselves. As soon as you begin the new lesson, they should rejoin the rest of the class for instruction.

# QUESTIONS AND ANSWERS ABOUT MOST DIFFICULT FIRST

*"How can I correct the work of the students who are trying the Most Difficult First problems, while simultaneously helping kids who are struggling?"*

As you walk around the classroom, giving assistance to students who need it, let those who are working on the Most Difficult First problems come to you. The first student to meet the criteria you've set becomes the checker for the rest of the period. Using her correct paper as the key, she goes to the students who indicate that they are done with the assignment. When she finds papers that are 80 to 100 percent accurate, and are neat and legible, she collects them to give to you at the end of the period.

Students are not allowed to correct any errors the checker discovers. Those who get more than one wrong are expected to complete the regular assignment, starting with the easier problems at the beginning of the sequence. In the first few days, they may come to you to protest, "I only made a careless mistake. I really know how to do it." Your reaction is always the same: "Exactly right. Better luck tomorrow! Please begin the rest of the assignment." Once students realize that you're not going to become the court of last resort, they will stop bothering you and start doing more careful work.

You'll notice I suggest that *you* correct everyone's paper until you find the checker for the day. My experience has been that gifted students are very competitive in this type of situation, and they may not be totally honest if you let them correct their own papers. They become very interested in how they are faring as compared to

their best buddy, and values get a little muddled. The checker is usually able to be more objective.

When the checker delivers the papers to you, simply put them in a stack to wait for tomorrow, when the rest of the papers come in. Then, as you enter the grades, do a quick spot check for accuracy. If you find an error that wasn't caught yesterday, that student loses the option of trying the Most Difficult First problems for the next assignment. Or you might ask your checkers to improve their accuracy.

As you can see, this strategy doesn't create any extra paperwork for you, nor do you spend any extra time entering grades. You can still do all of your bookkeeping at once, and you can be available to help your struggling students.

*"What will students do with the time they have left over after successfully completing the Most Difficult First problems?"*

It's perfectly acceptable for them to work on another subject, to do nothing, or even to daydream, as long as they don't bother anyone else and don't call attention to themselves. When we adults finish our work early, we appreciate having some free time. The same is true for our gifted students. There must be occasions in your classroom when kids can do whatever they like for short periods, even if you use this opportunity as a "carrot" to motivate students to get their work done.

However, we also want to demonstrate to our students that the world is full of exciting things to learn. Therefore, at the beginning of each unit, you may decide to collect some materials that represent enrichment activities for the concepts taught in the chapter. A large budget for math materials is not necessary. Most teachers' texts include suggestions for lots of enrichment activities. Some texts are accompanied by sets of enrichment dittos, or enrichment activity books. Parents, aides, student teachers, or students from higher grades may be able to help you get these activities ready for students to use. You might create an informal "Math Enrichment Center," using part of a shelf, an empty desk or table, or a learning center format. All materials in this center should extend the concepts being learned in the chapter and should be self-correcting.

It isn't necessary for you to correct and grade the enrichment work. The gifted students' grades, like everyone else's, should come from grade level work. If you want your gifted students to choose more challenging activities and to work on difficult problems for long periods of time, you must provide an environment where it is safe to risk being wrong. If you grade their enrichment activities and average those grades into their formal grade for that subject, they will resist any challenging work, telling you instead that they would rather do "what all the other kids are doing."

To help students keep track of the enrichment activities they do, you might provide a folder for each student who uses the center, so they can store their work in progress until they are able to return to a specific activity. As they finish the Most Difficult First problems, they may return to the center and get involved in one of the activities there.

Even if you set up an enrichment center, remember that it's still okay for students who qualify to work on another subject area, or to do nothing at all, if that is their choice.

### "Won't students who never qualify have self-esteem problems?"

When you carefully explain that *all* students will probably have to complete the entire assignment in order to master the concept, students will realize that they won't disappoint you by not qualifying for the Most Difficult First option. Naturally, those who do qualify shouldn't brag about it or tease the others.

Make certain that the activities available to qualifying students are also available at other times to all students. When class members perceive that only the most capable get to do the "fun stuff" on a regular basis, they are likely to resent it. Also make certain that your students understand this important concept: Equality means giving everyone equal opportunities to learn, *not* teaching everyone in exactly the same way.

When gifted students rarely or never get to work on highly challenging tasks, they slowly lose confidence in their ability to take on difficult projects. Failure to provide regular opportunities for them to struggle to learn is potentially damaging to *their* self-esteem.

### "What grade do students earn for doing only five problems?"

An "A." Demonstrating that they understand the material, rather than completing an arbitrary number of problems, should be sufficient proof that they have mastered a concept and are entitled to the "A" which represents mastery.

### "Shouldn't I be concerned if some students just 'vegetate' and waste their free time?"

Once we discover that some students don't need all of the time we designated to complete a task or activity, any remaining time should become their own, to spend however they choose. Subsequent chapters of this book describe strategies that require students to work on specific alternate activities when they earn free time in certain classes.

The real purpose of Most Difficult First is to help you see that gifted students can use free time without it being necessary for you to have replacement activities waiting to hand to them. Knowing this, you can begin to trust that it's okay to relinquish the need to control every minute of the time gifted students spend in school.

### "What if some of these students appear to need my help in choosing and doing the alternate activities?"

We've learned that gifted students who need help from the teacher can still be considered gifted. Bright students don't automatically come with independence skills. Just because they qualify for alternate activities doesn't necessarily mean that they know how to manage their time well, or use low voices, or stay on task. They need to be taught those skills. As you explain the guidelines for using free time, be sure to include information about whom to ask for help when you're busy, and what to do if they need to wait until you're free to assist them.

Some students have been known not to try available options because they don't want to lose contact with the teacher. Therefore, your plans should include spending some quality time with students who work with the alternate activities, teaching them how to use the enrichment materials, how to get assistance when they get stuck on a problem or activity they don't understand, how to keep track of their work, how to put things away, etc. Meet with them often to teach them these important skills—and to prove that they won't lose contact with you just because they choose to work more independently.

### "I'm using a whole language approach in reading, so I'm not teaching skills in isolation. The same is true in math, where we're focusing on problem-solving. How can I apply the Most Difficult First strategy in these cases?"

You might design an assessment instrument that gives students an opportunity to demonstrate mastery of concepts rather than isolated skills. Some students will still need differentiated activities that allow them to apply basic concepts to more complex activities. Also, Chapter 3 describes a Learning Contracts approach that might be more appropriate in your situation than Most Difficult First.

***"Is it okay for Most Difficult First to be the only differentiation method available to gifted students in my classroom?"***

No, because the students are still required to stay with the class during the entire lesson, and you may be spending many days teaching concepts they have already mastered. Most Difficult First is designed to be used *first*, so you can see that providing some unstructured time for gifted students is relatively easy to manage, and that most gifted students can be trusted to fill their free time with activities that are meaningful to them. When you have used this option for a few weeks, it will be time to move on to other management strategies described in subsequent chapters.

***"Does Most Difficult First work as well for other areas of the curriculum as it does for math?"***

Yes. Feel free to try this strategy with grammar, language mechanics, reading vocabulary, or other skill work. You might also want to try it with penmanship or vocabulary from curriculum areas such as social studies, science, or foreign language, if you teach these as separate skills. Don't include spelling for now. Chapter 2 presents a better strategy for teaching spelling.

# SUMMARY

This chapter describes the first strategy you should use as you begin to meet the learning needs of your gifted and talented students in the regular classroom. Students are allowed to try to complete the five or six most difficult problems or exercises first, before doing the rest of the assignment. When they successfully meet the criteria set by you, their "A" for that shorter assignment becomes their grade for the entire assignment, and they are free to use the time they have left over for activities of their own choosing. This strategy is designed for use with any content area that focuses on drill-and-practice, such as math, grammar, language mechanics, reading skills, or vocabulary.

Success with the shorter assignment provides the evidence you need that some students don't require as much practice as others. This strategy is remarkably successful with students who have become behavior problems and who may be refusing to do their work. Many behavior problems of gifted students are caused by boredom and frustration. When we are in power struggles with such students, we are really insisting that they do *our* work. Use Most Difficult First with your students and watch the amazing results.

## MORE RESOURCES FOR TEACHERS

- Reis, Sally M., Deborah K. Burns, and Joseph S. Renzulli. "Curriculum Compacting: A Process for Modifying Curriculum for High Ability Students." Storrs, CT: The National Research Center on the Gifted and Talented, 1992.

  One-hour training tape with accompanying teacher and facilitator guides.

- Starko, Alane. *It's About Time*. Mansfield Center, CT: Creative Learning Press, 1986.

  Strategies for compacting in all areas of the curriculum.

# COMPACTING THE CURRICULUM FOR MATH, GEOGRAPHY, LANGUAGE ARTS, SPELLING, AND READING SKILLS

## *"This is boring!"*

These words do not bring happiness to the hearts of teachers, although they are often in the minds of gifted students. It helps if students are specific in describing their boredom. That way, teachers know what to do about it.

I asked my gifted students to differentiate between "Boring A" situations ("I already know how to do that; could you please give me an opportunity to show you?") and "Boring B" situations ("At the present time, I do not know enough about this topic to be interested in it").

"Boring A" is most likely to occur in those subjects where the student has already learned the material in an earlier grade or from a source outside the classroom. Teaching methods that rely on scope-and-sequence charts or regular and cumulative review are not compatible with how gifted students learn, which is fast and forever. This chapter deals specifically with preventing "Boring A" situations from arising in your classroom.

"Boring B" is most likely to occur in subjects such as science, social studies, and literature, where even though the material may be new, gifted students can still learn it more quickly than their age peers. Chapter 4 describes techniques for meeting this challenge.

If we personalize the frustration gifted students feel with the regular curriculum, we can better understand their plight. Suppose you have signed up for an adult education course. You have chosen an advanced class that you hope will allow you to expand your skills in a particular area. Now suppose you discover at the first class meeting that a large percentage of the people in attendance obviously aren't ready for the advanced section, since they appear to have forgotten the basics. The instructor announces that she will spend several sessions reviewing those basics.

Your precious recreational time is limited. What will you do? Chances are you'll drop the course and seek a more suitable alternative. We adults are allowed to go elsewhere when it appears that our time will be wasted. However, gifted students in our schools don't have that option. When they think they are starting a year (or a class) filled with new and exciting content, then discover that it is going to begin with four to six weeks of intensive review of material they have already mastered, what they feel may be close to panic. Certainly chagrin; certainly an overwhelming sense of "Oh, no, here we go again!"

# STRATEGY: COMPACTING THE CURRICULUM

When teachers assume that the scope-and-sequence charts or curriculum guides they have been given must be applied to all students, this creates a situation that most gifted students find extremely difficult to cope with. Many of them, because they're teacher-pleasers, will go through the motions, do the work, produce some very respectable products, and easily get "A"'s. Others who are less compliant will go through the motions and do some of the work, but their work will be sloppy, messy, and careless. Of course, what they're saying is, "I know I've got to do this, but I just can't stand wasting all this time!" Still other gifted students will simply give up, reject any more repetition, and refuse to do something they know is not necessary. They will do nothing at all. Aaron, described in Chapter 1, pages 5-6, was once such a student.

The work that we plan for our students is really "our work." It doesn't become "their work" until it represents true learning for them. We need to find a way to allow students, as Dr. Joseph Renzulli explains, to "buy back" school time that we planned for them to "spend" in one way, so they can "spend" it another way. Renzulli calls this process *compacting*. Think of other contexts in which you use this term, and you'll probably come up with images of trash and garbage! Renzulli's method helps students deal with the part of the curriculum that represents "trash" to them because it is expendable. They can throw it away without missing it, and without incurring any academic harm.

Before we can start compacting, we need to determine what competencies certain students have and give them full credit for what they already know. Then we need to decide what to allow them to do with their "free time" so it doesn't become a burden to them, their classmates, or their teacher.

Curriculum for a gifted student should be compacted in those areas that represent the student's strengths. For example, if you have a student who is outstanding in mathematics and average in reading and writing, you would compact for him in math but not in reading and writing. We must guard against the practice of taking this gifted math student and making him use his earned free time to improve his perfor-

mance in his weaker subjects, such as poor handwriting. When students buy time for enrichment or alternate activities in a particular subject, they should be given opportunities to capitalize on those strengths through activities that enrich and extend their abilities. We must pay as much attention to their strengths as to their learning weaknesses.

Renzulli and Linda H. Smith created a record-keeping form called "The Compactor" to be used with students for whom compacting is done. You'll find a model Compactor on page 14.

# SCENARIO: ELIZABETH

Elizabeth had a learning disability and didn't appear to be very gifted. But she also had an avid interest in geography, maps, and national parks. During the year she was in my sixth grade, I took a class period to introduce an upcoming review unit on map skills. At the end of the period, Elizabeth came up to me, and we had the following conversation.

*ELIZABETH:* "You know, Mrs. Winebrenner, I know a lot about maps."

*ME:* "You do? How did that happen?"

*ELIZABETH:* "I don't know. I just love maps. I've always loved maps. Maps are just really interesting things to me."

*ME:* "What do you do with this love of maps?"

*ELIZABETH:* "Well, when my family goes on a trip, I get to plan the trip on the map."

*ME:* "No kidding! Where did you go last year?"

*ELIZABETH* (proudly): "Yellowstone National Park."

*ME:* "And how did you get there?"

Then Elizabeth did what I'm not sure I could do. She told me how she had gotten her family to Yellowstone—highway by highway, county by county, state by state, national monument by national monument.

*ME:* "Pretty impressive. Where did you go the year before?"

*ELIZABETH* (happily): "Great Smoky Mountains."

*ME:* "How did you get there?"

Once again, I heard the details.

*ME:* "Hmmm. I bet the prospect of spending six weeks reviewing basic map skills is not very appealing to you."

*ELIZABETH:* "I've thought about that."

*ME:* "I'll tell you what. I'll bring in the end-of-the-unit test tomorrow, and if you pass it with the equivalent of an 'A,' you won't have to do the map work that we're doing. You'll be able to spend your social studies time on a different activity of your choice."

*ELIZABETH* (smiling): "Thanks!"

Next, I did something I've learned to do routinely when offering "special consideration" to gifted students: I offered the same opportunity to everyone in the class. Sixteen of my 27 students volunteered to take the pretest.

The following day, I gave the pretest-takers a class period in social studies to complete the test, while the rest of us took an atlas tour of American geography. I told the students beforehand that if they did not receive an "A," their tests would not count. Six students completed the test. Two passed with "A"'s—Elizabeth and a student named James, described in the following scenario.

Elizabeth's Compactor, shown on page 16, is quite simple. The only subject for which she needed compacting was maps/geography. The words "map unit" in the far left column describe her area of strength. The center column shows how I documented her mastery by giving her as a pretest the same test she would have had to take at the end of the map unit. The far right column describes what she did with the time she "bought."

Elizabeth used the 45 minutes a day we spent on map work to do something that represented true learning for her. After discussing several options, she chose an activity in which she designed an imaginary country using papier-mâché. Because her learning disability prevented her from writing well, and she certainly would have been frustrated if she had been required to write down what she learned, she simply designed a country in which she located the population centers, the natural resources, the manufacturing centers, agricultural products, etc. When she was finished, she described her country to the class in a very interesting talk.

Did any of the other students say during the next six weeks, "How come Elizabeth doesn't have to do what we're doing?" No, because all students in our class had the same opportunity as Elizabeth to document their competency in that subject area, and most did not meet the prerequisite. Did any of them ask, "How come we can't do what Elizabeth's doing because it looks like fun?" Yes! In response to their interest, I used a similar activity for everyone as a culminating project for the map unit, and allowed Elizabeth to act as a "consultant" to the other students as they designed their own countries and made maps to show the results. Imagine the boost to Elizabeth's self-esteem as her self-image changed from that of a "needy" student with a learning disability to a student others turned to for help and advice.

## SCENARIO: JAMES

The other student who passed the map unit pretest was James. He was one of the most gifted writers I had ever taught, and at 11 years of age he was writing pieces I thought were worthy of much older students. He knew he didn't need the map work, but he thought it was rude to second-guess the teacher, and he never would have dreamed of asking for any kind of special consideration.

James had been an excellent student in the first quarter of the year, and I was surprised when his parents suggested that they might take him out of our school and try to send him to a special school for gifted children. When I asked them why, they replied that he was "kind of bored" with school and "didn't really enjoy" much of what he had to do. "As a matter of fact," his mother said, "his day really starts at about 3:45 P.M. It takes him 15 minutes to get home from school, and that's when he begins what he calls his 'real work.'"

"What is his 'real work'?" I asked.

"He's writing a book," she replied.

James was indeed writing a book. It was called "The Anatomy, Physiology, and Cetera of the Human Body by James T. Myers, Age 11." He was printing it in pencil in two columns to resemble a textbook, and illustrating it himself. Some of his pictures were very technical, similar to those found in an anatomy textbook. Others were cartoons where, for example, little men in green eye shades and sleeve protectors ran around shouting orders to each other to communicate the message of the DNA molecule. Each chapter was on a different system of the human body, and James's incredible sense of humor was rampant throughout.

In James's mind, he came to school to do the work the teacher and the school had decided he

## THE COMPACTOR
### Joseph Renzulli & Linda H. Smith

**Student's Name:** _____

| Areas of Strength | Documenting Mastery | Alternate Activities |
|---|---|---|
|  |  |  |
|  |  |  |
|  |  |  |
|  |  |  |

should do, even if he really didn't need to do it. But the work that was really meaningful to him—the work that represented true learning—didn't begin until he got home.

I asked the parents to give me a few weeks to try to solve the problem. During that time,

---

## HOW TO USE THE COMPACTOR

1. Provide one Compactor for each student. You may need to make a new one each month for a student who requires a great deal of compacting.

2. Use the Compactor to record all modifications in curriculum.

   • In the far left column, record the student's areas of strength, one per box.

   • In the center column, describe the methods used to document the student's mastery of skill, competency, chapter, concept, or unit.

   • In the far right column, describe the activities the student will be engaged in while the rest of the class is doing grade level work.

   Alternate activities are usually drawn from the same subject area from which the student "bought" the time. Sometimes, however, they may represent activities from different subject areas, and sometimes they may be ongoing projects related to a student's passionate interest.

3. Keep a folder for each student for whom you compact the curriculum. Include all pretests and other pertinent data, with dates; all Compactors; and brief records of alternate activities.

## CAUTION

• NEVER use the time a student buys from a strength area to remediate a learning weakness.

• ALWAYS allow students to enjoy extended activities in their areas of strength.

---

I pretested James in every single area of his strength. As you look at his Compactor on page 16, you can see that James was ultimately able to "buy back" almost half of every school day. During that time, he went off to a corner he had named his "office" to work on his book.

The only time that James needed formal instruction in spelling, language arts, writing, etc., was when I, as the new editor of his manuscript, discovered some kind of consistent errors. He would attend a lesson only when other class members were learning about a concept he needed to master. For his spelling, he kept a list of the words he frequently misspelled in his manuscript, and when he accumulated ten or so, he studied those and had someone give him a test on Friday, when the class took a final test in spelling. (I call this method *functional spelling,* since it helps students learn the words they need to use to function well in their writing.)

By earning an "A" on the map unit pretest, James bought himself an additional six weeks of social studies time. He would have been eligible to buy some time in science, but James adored the science teacher and the special science program, so compacting in science was not an option. Art was also taught by a separate teacher, and was not included in his compacting plan.

James's Compactor shows exactly where the time came from to work on his book in school. Since he was obviously gifted in all of the language arts by virtue of his superior writing ability, he took pretests only of *review* units. For further evidence, his writing portfolio, with collected writings since the beginning of the year, clearly documented his writing ability and served as additional evidence of his mastery of grade level competencies.

James was also able to buy time from our whole language reading program, because he was reading technical material to support the research on his book. Had we been using a traditional reading program, I would have provided pretests to document his mastery of the skills and vocabulary.

James's compacting plan was unique because he spent all of the time he bought working on his book. He did not do enrichment work in the same curriculum areas from which he bought the time—at least, not strictly speaking. Because work on his book covered so many curriculum areas, this was not a problem. I made a professional call that the time he bought from social studies by earning an "A" on the map unit pretest could be spent working on his book. Of course, I also gave him the option to choose from the alternatives available to Elizabeth, but he happily declined.

## THE COMPACTOR
### Joseph Renzulli & Linda H. Smith

**Student's Name:** *Elizabeth*

| Areas of Strength | Documenting Mastery | Alternate Activities |
|---|---|---|
| *Map unit* | *Achieved "A" on pretest* | *Will create a country from papier-mâché*<br><br>*Will present report to class*<br><br>*Will "consult" with other students to help them create their own countries* |
| | | |
| | | |
| | | |

## THE COMPACTOR
### Joseph Renzulli & Linda H. Smith

**Student's Name:** *James*

| Areas of Strength | Documenting Mastery | Alternate Activities |
|---|---|---|
| *Language arts, spelling, writing, grammar, mechanics* | *Pretest results of "A" on review tests*<br><br>*Portfolio collection of exceptional writing* | *Will write his book when class is working on skills he has already mastered* |
| *Reading* | *Pretest results of "A" on review tests of skills and vocabulary* | *Will read to gather research for his book*<br><br>*Will write his book*<br><br>*Will join class for two group novels* |
| *Maps* | *Pretest results of "A"* | *Will write his book INSTEAD of doing enrichment activities in map-related work. Was given options and chose this.* |
| | | |

How many students asked, "Why doesn't James have to do the work we're doing?" None, because I had described the criteria James had to meet before buying class time to write his book, and I had offered the same opportunity to anyone else who might request it. How many asked, "Why can't we write books, too?" Several, and their interest encouraged me to create opportunities for them to do just that.

# SCENARIO: ARDITH

We all know students who master spelling words before a particular week's lesson is presented. Some teachers dictate a voluntary pretest in spelling every Monday, and those students who earn an "A" do not have to do any of the workbook exercises. Instead, the students may choose from among several alternate activities, or buy back time to do more actual reading and quality writing.

Ardith, a bright third grader, had consistently earned "A"'s on every spelling test, including pretests. Her Compactor is shown below. I gave Ardith a list of alternate spelling activities to choose from. You'll find a reproducible list to use with your students on page 18.

Ardith was not the only student who earned "A"'s on her spelling pretests. Like many other students in my class who chose to work on alternate spelling activities, she often went with activity #1: "Working with a partner who also passed the pretest, find 10 unfamiliar words from glossaries of books in our room. Learn their meanings and spellings. You and your partner may agree on 10 words, each choosing 5. You will give each other your final spelling test." Students searched the glossaries of their literature, reading, social studies, and/or science books for unfamiliar words. On Fridays, while I dictated a test to the whole class as a post-test, these students dictated their words to their partners and discussed their meanings. Another popular option was activity #2, which instructed students to study words they consistently misspelled in their own writing. They were responsible for learning the spelling and the meaning of each word on their list. As noted earlier, I call this *functional spelling*.

If you are teaching from a whole language perspective, you may not be treating spelling as

---

### THE COMPACTOR
#### Joseph Renzulli & Linda H. Smith

**Student's Name:** _Ardith_

| Areas of Strength | Documenting Mastery | Alternate Activities |
|---|---|---|
| Spelling | Passed pretest with "A" | Will choose from list of alternate spelling activities OR write ongoing stories, poems, etc. |
|  |  |  |
|  |  |  |
|  |  |  |

# ALTERNATE SPELLING ACTIVITIES

If you pass a spelling pretest with a score of 90 percent or higher, *you do not have to complete the workbook activities OR take a final test.* You may choose to work on one or more of these alternate activities.

## Using New Words

1. Working with a partner who also passed the pretest, find 10 unfamiliar words from glossaries of books in our room. Learn their meanings and spellings. You and your partner may agree on 10 words, each choosing 5. You will give each other your final spelling test. For the test, one partner says a word out loud. The other partner gives an acceptable meaning for the word, then writes down the spelling. Do this for the first five words, then switch for the last five words. Check each others' spelling.

2. Keep track of words you misspell in your own writing. Learn them when you have collected 5 words.

*For both activities #1 and #2, misspelled words will be moved to next week's list. Remember that you are learning to spell for MASTERY.*

## Using Regular or Alternate Words

3. Use all the words to create as few sentences as possible.

4. Create a crossword puzzle on graph paper. Include an answer key.

5. Learn the words in a foreign language. Create sentences with the words.

6. Create several categories into which all the words can fit. Regroup them into different categories.

7. Create greeting card messages or rebus pictures.

8. Create an original spelling game.

9. Create riddles with the words as the answers.

10. Write an advertisement using as many of the words as you can.

11. Use all of the words in an original story.

12. Create alliterative sentences using the words.

13. Using a thesaurus, find synonyms and antonyms for the words, and use them in sentences.

14. Change the initial or middle consonants to create other words. Or keep the consonants the same and change vowels to form other words.

15. Create analogies using the words. (Example: "heart" is to "body" what "motor" is to "lawn mower.")

16. Using an unabridged dictionary, locate and describe the history of each word (its *etymology*). Create flow charts to show how the meaning has changed over time.

17. Come up with your own activity. Discuss it with the teacher.

a separate subject. You are probably integrating it into other whole language activities, and that's fine. To use the compacting strategy, simply transfer it to another subject in which students are required to do tasks that some of them may not need to do.

# QUESTIONS AND ANSWERS ABOUT COMPACTING THE CURRICULUM

*"Do I have to keep a Compactor for every student who works on differentiated activities during time bought from the regular curriculum?"*

It's always a good idea to keep a brief record of changes you make from the regular curriculum for any student, gifted or otherwise, who needs differentiation. Accountability is a concern in education today, and if we choose to deviate from accepted practices, we should have records to document that we are following a specific plan and know what we're doing. Although I have not included Compactors for all of the students described in this book, I did in fact keep careful records of what they were doing, and I advise you to do the same.

*"Won't it harm the students not to do the spelling workbook?"*

The idea of compacting the spelling curriculum causes anxiety among some teachers. They feel that the curriculum publishers "must know what they're doing" and "there must be some important reason why the book is teaching a certain rule at a certain time." If you're worried that some of your students won't learn a particular rule because they are working on alternate activities, ask them to find words from their sources that demonstrate that rule. For example, when the spelling book teaches compound words, tell the students to create their lists with compound words. When the book introduces the *schwa* sound, ask them to find words that have the *schwa* sound in them, and draw a box or circle around the syllable illustrating the sound. The students will still be learning the same concept as the rest of the class. They'll just be doing it with words that are challenging to them.

*"What grade do the students earn in spelling when a unit is compacted?"*

The "A" they earned on the pretest. The words on their independent lists are not graded; they are simply charted in some way. For example, you might provide a bar graph to show how many words they have studied and how many words they spelled correctly on the final test. Any words they don't get right are transferred to their next list. This teaches the students that one continues to study a word until mastery is achieved.

*"What if some students sneak their spelling books home on Friday and cram for the test over the weekend? Won't they forget very quickly how to spell the words?"*

Under present circumstances, when do students "sneak" their spelling books home to study? The answer is Thursday night or never! So let them sneak their spelling books home. How can it hurt your public relations if parents see their kids calling up their friends on the weekend and begging them to come over so they can study spelling?

You may observe that some kids do very well on spelling tests, but seem unable to transfer good spelling to their written work. If this happens with the pretest method, we know it can happen anyway using a traditional format for spelling, so let's not blame the pretest method. Use the functional spelling approach to address this problem.

*"What if a terrible speller passes the pretest?"*

Congratulate him and let him pretend that he's a great speller for one week, as he works with other kids on the alternate activities he qualified for.

*"Won't kids feel bad if they take the pretest and don't meet the criteria for passing?"*

It helps if you leave some room for error. I usually allow students to pass the pretest if they spell at least 18 out of 20 words correctly. Most students understand that it's the teacher's job to make individual adjustments to the regular content for certain students for a variety of reasons. They may need some reassurance from you that you really don't expect them to pass the test, because if everyone knew what you were planning to teach this year, you'd be out of a job!

As teachers, we meet with few objections when the modifications we make benefit struggling students. We need to offer the same consideration to students at the top end, because their learning needs are just as different as those of students who may be operating below grade level expectations. Justice Felix Frankfurter said it best when he observed, "There is nothing so unequal as the equal treatment of unequals." Equality in education has never meant that all students should be treated the same. Rather, it means that all students should enjoy equal opportunities to actualize their learning potential.

*"I'm using a whole language program, and we don't use a regular spelling book. Will these methods work for me?"*

Yes, they will. You may find that the functional spelling approach works best. Have your students make a list of the words they misspell in their other assignments. When their list numbers 6-10 words, they should study those words and find someone to test them on those words. Any words that are misspelled on the functional spelling test are transferred to the beginning of the next list.

# SUMMARY

The three scenarios presented in this chapter illustrate what compacting is all about. For "Boring A" subjects, where it's likely that some students have learned and mastered the material at an earlier time, compacting simply means 1) finding the students' areas of strength, 2) pretesting to determine which of the concepts you're about to teach they already know, and 3) physically excusing them from wasting their time on repetition. Compacting frees them to use that time for work that is more meaningful to them.

For gifted students, there really is no such thing as "extra credit." The only students who might benefit from extra credit are those who *need the credit*—not those who are already earning high grades. Why, then, when we think "extra credit," do we usually assume that students first have to complete their regular work before going on to the "good stuff"? Gifted students should have frequent and consistent opportunities to demonstrate prior knowledge and use their school time for their "real work": work that represents true learning and actual struggle for them. Otherwise, these students will be robbed of the chance to experience that learning *is* struggle, and that the world will value them even if they have to struggle to learn.

When you offer pretest opportunities for "Boring A" situations, and use the Compactor to keep accurate records of the adaptations you design for qualifying students, you will have all the evidence you need to reassure anxious parents or administrators that the gifted students are not "skipping" important work. Rather, as your

records will show, these students will have replaced previously mastered concepts with work that represents real learning for them.

Compacting works best for spelling, grammar, language arts exercises, vocabulary, handwriting, number facts, math, or any other content that some students might have previously mastered. There are no significant negative effects that would make it risky for you to try this strategy; the positive effects are too numerous to list. After reading this chapter, you should be ready to begin compacting for several students you suspect would benefit from it. Be sure to keep a separate folder for each eligible student, containing the Compactor and all dated pretests and other assessment records.

---

# MORE RESOURCES FOR TEACHERS

- Reis, Sally M., Deborah K. Burns, and Joseph S. Renzulli. "Curriculum Compacting: A Process for Modifying Curriculum for High Ability Students." Storrs, CT: The National Research Center on the Gifted and Talented, 1992.

    One-hour training tape with accompanying teacher and facilitator guides.

- Renzulli, Joseph, ed. *Systems and Models for Developing Programs for the Gifted and Talented.* Mansfield Center, CT: Creative Learning Press, 1986.

    Descriptions of many types of gifted program options at all grade levels.

- Renzulli, Joseph, and Sally Reis. *The Schoolwide Enrichment Model.* Mansfield Center, CT: Creative Learning Press, 1985.

    How to bring enrichment opportunities to all students in a school.

- Starko, Alane. *It's About Time.* Mansfield Center, CT: Creative Learning Press, 1986.

    Strategies for compacting in all areas of the curriculum.

# LEARNING CONTRACTS THAT REALLY WORK

**W**hile trying out the Most Difficult First strategy described in Chapter 1, you may notice some flaws in using that strategy exclusively. First, gifted students still have to attend the class for the teaching of the concepts they may have already mastered, and are not allowed to demonstrate mastery until the homework portion is begun. Secondly, students may need more structure regarding their use of the time they buy back. The method of choice for solving these problems is the learning contract.

## SCENARIO: JULIE

Julie was a fifth-grade student who had been getting consistent "A"'s in her daily math work and on her quizzes and tests. She appeared to remember most of what she had learned in previous grades, and she also seemed to catch on quickly to new concepts. However, she began to develop some distracting behaviors during math class. She stared out the window, occasionally hummed softly, and was frequently found writing notes to friends. It became obvious that part of her problem was boredom with the pace and depth of the fifth-grade math curriculum.

The learning contract option was very appealing to her. When she passed the pretest for the fractions chapter with an acceptable score—a condition for being allowed to work on contract—I gave her the contract shown on page 22. I checked pages 61, 64, and 68 because they taught concepts Julie had not yet mastered. I also checked page 66 to give her more practice in word problems, and page 70 so I could document that she still remembered previously taught concepts. Like all students on contract, she would have to take the post-test to make sure that her pretest results did not reflect "cramming" or parental assistance.

Julie knew from her contract that she would have to be with the class six times during the chapter, when we learned the material on the pages checked on her contract. She also knew not to work on the checked pages until she joined the class. If she rushed ahead and completed the pages before the class reached them, she might be denied the opportunity to pretest for the next chapter. Julie's behavior became more task-oriented, and she enjoyed the freedom she felt she had gained from the contract system.

---

## ★ IMPORTANT ★

Even if you have used learning contracts before and vowed "never again," don't skip this chapter! The strategy described here represents an easy way to individualize learning for gifted students while still maintaining tight control over areas in which they need instruction.

All of the glitches that usually accompany the use of contracts have been worked out. No more will long lines of students form, waiting for your help. No more will you need to "tutor on the run" instead of teaching purposefully. No more will students race one another to see who can finish the contract first. *I promise.* Please read on.

---

## MATH CONTRACT
### FRACTIONS

NAME: _Julie_

| ✓ | Page/Concept | ✓ | Page/Concept | ✓ | Page/Concept |
|---|---|---|---|---|---|
|   | 60 | ✓ | 64 | ✓ | 68 |
| ✓ | 61 |   | 65 |   | 69 |
|   | 62 | ✓ | 66-Word Problems | ✓ | 70-Review (even only) |
|   | 63 |   | 67 | ✓ | Post-test |

..................................................................................................

ENRICHMENT OPTIONS:    _Choose tasks about fractions_

Special instructions

Versa-Tiles  _____     ____ ____ ____ ____ ____ ____ ____ ____

Write Story Problems  _____     ____ ____ ____ ____ ____ ____ ____ ____

Cross Number Puzzles  _____     ____ ____ ____ ____ ____ ____ ____ ____

YOUR IDEA:

_____     ____ ____ ____ ____ ____ ____ ____ ____

..................................................................................................

### WORKING CONDITIONS

1. No talking to teacher while teacher is teaching

2. When you need help & teacher is busy, ask someone else

3. If no one can help you right away, keep trying yourself or go on to something else

4. If you must go in and out of the room, do it quietly

5. Don't bother anyone else

6. Don't call attention to yourself

Teacher's signature _____

Student's signature _____

---

# STRATEGY:
# THE LEARNING CONTRACT

Start by preparing a master contract for each chapter. You'll find a reproducible Learning Contract form on page 24.* Announce to the class:

"At the beginning of each chapter, a full class period will be given for students who want to take a pretest. Those who earn a 'B' or higher

on the pretest may work through the chapter on a contract system. Those who know they will need more help with the chapter may use the pretest time to work on 'fun stuff'— enrichment activities for concepts you have

---

*For some of the newer textbooks that stress critical thinking and problem-solving, it may not be possible to set up the contract exactly the way it is shown on the form. Elena's scenario on pages 26 and 29 addresses this situation. This chapter also describes other ways to customize the learning contract.

previously mastered. I'll be available to help you with the enrichment activities."

Given this introduction, everyone looks forward to pretest day. Students who want to qualify for a contract get the chance to do so. Students who wouldn't be eligible for a contract get teacher-directed time to work on exciting activities. Gifted students don't mind missing this enrichment day because, if they become eligible for a contract, they'll have lots of opportunities for "fun stuff" while the rest of the class is learning material from the textbook.

If the book you are using includes both a chapter review and a chapter test, use whichever one is most comprehensive. Correct the pretest papers and prepare contracts for students who achieve a "B" or higher. Point out that the others have demonstrated that they need your assistance with the concepts covered in the chapter, so it makes sense that they will work under your direction. Emphasize that not qualifying for a contract doesn't result in any loss of status or regard from you.

Tell the contract students that they must attend the regular instructional classes only on days when the pages checked on their contracts are being taught. (Most teachers' editions indicate the page on which each concept is taught, and it becomes a simple matter to list and check the appropriate pages on each student's contract.) On other days, the students will work on related enrichment activities.

The feature that makes this contract system different from most others is that students on contract are *never* allowed to work on pages from the chapter until the entire class is being taught those concepts by you, the teacher. In other words, there is no chance for your students to race one another to see who completes the contract first.

Note that Julie's contract lists several enrichment options.* To simplify contract management, you may decide to offer just one option for the first chapter of a unit, add a second option for the second chapter, and so on. Some teachers instruct

their students to choose activities that reinforce the concepts covered in the chapter. Other teachers allow students to choose any activity, as long as it's related to the subject being taught. Students record their choices on the contract.

Introduce the enrichment materials carefully, and coach the students personally on how to use them. If your class perceives that students on contract rarely get the chance to work with you, they may stop taking the pretests. You should plan to work with the contract group at least twice each week, explaining how to use the enrichment materials and demonstrating different problem-solving techniques.

The last option on your list should invite students to create their own alternate activity, with permission from you. Several teachers have had success encouraging students on contract to create learning activities for the rest of the class. This gives everyone the chance to enjoy extension activities on a regular basis, and to explore ideas they may not otherwise be exposed to. In some classrooms, this has served as a springboard for designing a course of study that allows all students to spend more time on critical thinking and problem-solving activities, applying their skills in more challenging ways than traditional textbook drill-and-practice.

Don't indicate on the contract which enrichment activities the students should do, and don't expect them to complete an entire activity each day. Since the activities are supposed to be challenging, your most important task is to encourage students to persevere even when they become frustrated. Consider letting students work together, giving one another the support and motivation they need to persist with difficult activities instead of choosing the easiest ones available. Let it be known that you will continue to value each student's intelligence, even if he or she must work hard to master a concept or task. Many gifted students have erroneously concluded that smart means quick, and if they are seen struggling with a task or taking longer than usual to complete an activity, people might conclude that they aren't so smart after all.

The contract should also describe the students' "working conditions"—rules of behavior. Negotiate these with the group during your first meeting, perhaps during a time when the other students are doing work that doesn't require your presence. Some conditions to include are:

1. You will not talk to the teacher when the teacher is teaching.

---

*Versa-Tiles, listed among the enrichment options on the sample contract, are a self-correcting enrichment activity. Students work with problem books and a tray of plastic tiles. When they finish a problem set, they can check to see if they did the work correctly by closing the lid of the tile tray, turning the tray upside down, and comparing the picture their solutions have created with the answer key picture in the problem book. Students can choose from many types of problems, all of which use the tile tray to display answers. Versa-Tiles are available from Educational Teaching Aids; see Appendix C, page 151.

# LEARNING CONTRACT

CHAPTER: _____

NAME: _____

| ✓ | Page/Concept | ✓ | Page/Concept | ✓ | Page/Concept |
|---|---|---|---|---|---|
| ____ | _____ | ____ | _____ | ____ | _____ |
| ____ | _____ | ____ | _____ | ____ | _____ |
| ____ | _____ | ____ | _____ | ____ | _____ |
| ____ | _____ | ____ | _____ | ____ | _____ |

• • • • • • • • • • • • • • • • • • • • • • • • • • • • • • • • • • • • • • • • • • •

ENRICHMENT OPTIONS: _____

Special instructions

_____  _____  _____  _____  _____  _____

_____  _____  _____  _____  _____  _____

_____  _____  _____  _____  _____  _____

YOUR IDEA:

_____  _____  _____  _____  _____  _____

• • • • • • • • • • • • • • • • • • • • • • • • • • • • • • • • • • • • • • • • • • •

## WORKING CONDITIONS

_____

_____

_____

_____

_____

Teacher's signature _____

Student's signature _____

2. When you need help and the teacher is busy...*(agree on an acceptable behavior)*.

3. If no one can help you right away, you may...*(agree on an acceptable behavior)* while waiting for the teacher to become available.

4. You are expected to move noiselessly in and out of the classroom.

5. Don't bother anyone else.

6. Don't call attention to yourself.

---

# HOW TO USE THE LEARNING CONTRACT

1. Collect enrichment materials that extend concepts taught in the chapter.
   - Check the teacher's manual for ideas.
   - Enlist parents' help to create materials.
   - Provide answer keys. All materials should be self-correcting.

2. Design a master contract for each chapter.
   - In the top third, list the relevant text page numbers or concepts, with check-off spaces.
   - In the middle third, list the enrichment options (alternate activities), with spaces for students to record their progress.
   - In the bottom third, specify the agreed-upon working conditions. (Or wait until completing step #7 below.)

3. Make a pretest or other type of assessment available when each new chapter or unit begins.

4. Correct the assessment activity. Give contracts to those students who demonstrate mastery of 80–85% of the planned curriculum.

5. Prepare contracts for qualified students.
   - Check pages or concepts they have *not* mastered and others you want them to do.
   - Tell the students they are not allowed to work on the checked items until you teach them to the whole class.
   - Explain that they will work on alternate enrichment activities when the class is learning things they have already mastered.

6. Prepare the middle part of the contract with a menu of enrichment and extension activities.
   - Start with one or two options for the first unit; add others cumulatively.
   - Always include several Free Choice options.

7. Meet with the students on contract as a group.
   - Explain contract procedures.
   - Explain that students may choose from these activities on days when they are excused from participating in a particular lesson.
   - Demonstrate the new enrichment activity for each unit. Students can help each other learn about activities from previous units.
   - Show students how to keep track of the work they do.
   - Explain the working conditions listed on the bottom of the contract. (Some teachers display a "Working Conditions Chart" in the room instead of having to include the conditions on all contracts.)

8. Continue to meet with the students on contract.
   - Plan to meet at least twice a week, or more often as necessary.
   - Work with the students to help them develop the skills and independence they need to use the enrichment materials.
   - Get student feedback about the enrichment options.

9. Evaluate the work of students on contract.
   - Grades should only reflect grade level work. Enrichment work should not be averaged in or students will resist it.
   - Alternate methods of assessment are perfectly acceptable.

If you prefer, you may use the reproducible Working Conditions form found on page 32.

Both you and the student should sign the contract. This makes it feel like a formal agreement, with obligations and responsibilities for all.

Before giving the contract to the student, indicate in your grade book which textbook pages you have checked for him or her. One way to do this is by drawing a colored box around the square that indicates a specific page in the text. As you begin each class, you can tell at a glance which students are supposed to be there for instruction, and which will be working on alternate activities.

Where should the contract students work while you are teaching the rest of the class? Some teachers rearrange the seating chart for each chapter they teach, keeping the students who aren't on contract in the part of the room where they do their direct teaching, and grouping those who are on contract in an "enrichment center" in another part of the room. In some schools, the contract students spend their "enrichment days" in another room, under the direction of a resource person such as a media center specialist or a librarian.

The enrichment center may be formal or informal, as you choose. It should contain *self-correcting* activities that extend and enrich concepts being taught in the corresponding chapter. It should contain a place for students to store their work when they leave the center. One system that works well is a plastic crate that accommodates hanging file folders. Students leave their work in progress in their folder to await their return.

To assign a grade to a contract student, average all the work the student has done in the chapter *from the text only*—the same as for non-contract students. You may supervise or discuss the enrichment work, but don't grade it. This encourages students to take the risks associated with tackling challenging new problems. If your students refuse to do work without getting grades, arrange some credit for following the working conditions, persisting with difficult tasks for more than one day, or other behaviors you want to encourage.

## CUSTOMIZING THE LEARNING CONTRACT

Because the basic concept of the learning contract is so widely applicable—and because learning contracts are so easy to use, now that the bugs have been worked out—it becomes a simple matter to customize this strategy to meet the needs of individual students. Following are several scenarios describing particular students and the contracts that were invented just for them. You may find some of these useful for your purposes in their present form, or you may use them as starting points for your own customized learning contracts.

## SCENARIO: DIMITRI

Dimitri passed the pretests for several math chapters with 100 percent accuracy. I had him do some pages in the text that represented more complex concepts, and he completed those with zero errors. Clearly, here was a student who needed math instruction at a higher grade level. I designed a special contract for Dimitri, shown on page 27. This Contract for Accelerated Learning can be used to document mastery of 95-100 percent on an entire chapter, in which case the student is not required to complete any pages in that chapter.

## SCENARIO: ROBERTO

Roberto was a first grader who was very precocious in math. He usually finished all tasks quickly, then got into trouble by "helping" other students in his inimitable, bossy way. His teacher designed a hands-on math program that focused on teaching critical thinking and problem-solving through manipulatives. Because this program was not skill-based, a master contract like the one on page 24 was not appropriate. Yet Roberto needed opportunities to work with more complex tasks that would engage his attention for longer periods of time, and his teacher needed a way to document his work.

Roberto's learning contract is shown on page 28. Once his teacher was satisfied that Roberto understood a specific concept with less practice and repetition than his age peers, Roberto was able to work on tasks that extended and enriched the basic concept.

## SCENARIO: ELENA

Elena's class was using a newer math text that stressed critical thinking and problem-solving and didn't lend itself to the traditional learning contract approach. Her teacher had been told to teach the entire class as one group, and she was having trouble keeping the gifted students

## CONTRACT FOR ACCELERATED LEARNING

Student's Name: _Dimitri_

| | | |
|---|---|---|
| _____ Chapter One | _____ Chapter Four | _____ Chapter Seven |
| _____ Chapter Two | _____ Chapter Five | _____ Chapter Eight |
| _____ Chapter Three | _____ Chapter Six | _____ Chapter Nine |

| Chapter # and Concept | Enrichment | Acceleration |
|---|---|---|
| | | |
| | | |
| | | |

Teacher's signature _____    Student's signature _____

# HOW TO USE THE CONTRACT FOR ACCELERATED LEARNING

1. Give very precocious students the end-of-chapter tests for as many chapters as they can demonstrate mastery with a score of 95-100 percent. These tests may be taken out of sequence, since some students will have mastered concepts here and there throughout the text.

2. On the top part of the contract, record the dates on which mastery was documented. Date all tests and keep them in the student's compacting folder.

3. On the bottom part of the contract, keep track of the activities or program changes you choose for the student.

   • If you choose enrichment, or if acceleration is not an option in your school, describe the types of activities the student will be engaged in.

   • If you choose acceleration, see #4 below.

4. For students who demonstrate mastery of a great deal of grade level work, some acceleration of content is indicated. There are two ways to accomplish this:

   • by having the student attend the class in another grade, and/or

   • by having the student work on advanced materials in your classroom.

## CAUTION

• Accelerated students should *never* use the actual materials used in a subsequent grade level, to avoid the very real possibility of repetition in the future. The only exception is if a separate class is formed for students accelerated in math, and a scope-and-sequence is developed that guarantees that these students will not repeat the use of texts, even if they fail to remain in the accelerated class.

• *Never* make acceleration arrangements without informing the other interested parties, such as parents, other teachers, and administrators. Any acceleration of content requires careful planning beyond the current school year. For example, where will the accelerated student go next? Is the middle school or high school prepared to admit a youthful, precocious student? Questions like these must be addressed before you choose acceleration for a particular student.

## CONTRACT FOR HANDS-ON MATH PROGRAM

Student's Name: _Roberto_ _____

| _____ Sorting | _____ Attributes | _____ Estimating |
| _____ Classifying | _____ Measurement | _____ Rote counting |
| _____ Patterning | _____ Graphing | _____ Place value |
| _____ Number concepts | | |

Methods used to document mastery of concepts listed above: _____

_____

_____

Enrichment and extension opportunities for concepts listed above:

| DATE | ACTIVITY |
|---|---|
| | |

Teacher's signature _____  Student's signature _____

# HOW TO USE THE CONTRACT FOR HANDS-ON LEARNING

1. On the top part of the contract, list the concepts the program will teach.

   - Use the ideas shown in the example or substitute your own.
   - Include all of the concepts that will be covered in the unit of study.

2. Plan tasks that are designed to extend basic concepts. Start by conducting a formal or informal assessment of the student's abilities.

   - Use checklists or tests provided by textbook publishers.
   - Set up "stations" at which the student can demonstrate previous mastery of concepts.

   - Observe the student's learning behavior during tasks.
   - Record information from your tests or observations on the top part of the contract.

3. Provide opportunities for the student to work on alternate activities after demonstrating competency with specific concepts.

4. On the bottom part of the contract, record the alternate activities. Or list several choices and have the student keep track of those he or she does, much the same way the choices are listed on Julie's contract on page 22.

interested while the rest of the class went over the same concept several times. Because Elena was a teacher-pleaser, she never complained. However, her parents were hinting that they didn't think their daughter was being adequately challenged.

Elena's teacher planned activities to extend the basic problem-solving experiences for highly capable math students, and created a special Contract for Math Program with Problem-Solving Focus, shown on page 30. This contract made it easy to meet the differentiated learning needs of students like Elena. Even when all students are working on similar problem-solving strategies, the problems themselves should be different, reflecting the degree of difficulty each student is capable of handling.

## SCENARIO: LEANDRA

Leandra was reading several years ahead of her age peers. Her writing was sophisticated and colorful. Her class was using a basal reader approach for reading, and a language arts text for grammar, mechanics, and punctuation practice. Her teacher recognized that it was not necessary for Leandra to complete all the skill-and-practice assignments at grade level, and she created the contract shown on page 31 to allow Leandra to spend more time doing what she truly loved: reading and writing.

You'll notice that this contract lists no specific activities as enrichment options, since there is no such thing as "gifted grammar." Students may spend the time they buy reading books they have chosen, and/or writing and revising ongoing pieces. It's very important to realize that it isn't necessary to provide paper-and-pencil activities to replace those activities students have been excused from doing. The students should have much freedom of choice in how they spend the time they buy. For information on compacting and differentiation for reading and whole language programs, see Chapter 7.

## QUESTIONS AND ANSWERS ABOUT LEARNING CONTRACTS

*"What happens when students on contract don't join the group for instruction on the days they're supposed to?"*

Just because students are gifted doesn't mean they are well-organized or totally responsible. They

have to be *taught* those skills. Before I give a student a contract, I draw a red box around the pages in my grade book that I have checked for that student to do. Each day, when I have announced or written on the board which page we are doing for the daily lesson, I ask the contract students to check to see if they should be with us for that lesson. For a few weeks, I may write their names on the board to help them get in the habit of noticing when they should attend the class. When I notice that someone who should be with the group is absent, I gently remind all of the contract students to check their contracts again. If the problem persists, I ask the particular student to return to the group for the remainder of the chapter. Of course, all students receive another chance to become eligible for a contract for the next chapter.

*"What will I do if the students on contract waste time or disturb the class on the days they are working on enrichment activities?"*

You might speak to the students once or twice, referring them to the written working conditions that are part of their contract. You might meet with them to make sure they understand how to do the enrichment activities, and to find out if the activities are proving to be unrealistically difficult. You might check to make sure you're spending enough time with the students on contract, so they don't feel they've lost touch with you. When all else fails, you may have to advise the students to rejoin the class for the rest of the chapter. Once again, reassure them that they will have the chance to qualify for a contract for the next chapter.

Some teachers prefer to use one set of working conditions for all types of contracts—a generally applicable statement of acceptable and unacceptable behaviors. See page 32 for an example you can copy and attach to your students' contracts.

*"Will correcting work for the students on contract create a lot of paperwork for me?"*

ALL work in the enrichment center should be self-correcting. Provide answer keys whenever possible.

The work that students on contract do with the class as a whole is corrected at the same time as everyone else's work, and their grades are entered into your grade book at the same time. In other words, there should be little or no extra paperwork for you to do. But if you need help, consider asking for parent or student volunteers. Be sure to emphasize the importance of confidentiality.

To save even more on paperwork, it may not be necessary to keep Compactors for students on

## CONTRACT FOR MATH PROGRAM WITH PROBLEM-SOLVING FOCUS

Student's Name: _Elena_

_____ Make tables or graphs      _____ Estimate first, check later      _____ Use objects; manipulatives

_____ Make pictures              _____ Create an organized list         _____ Use logical reading

_____ Make diagrams              _____ Work backwards                   _____ Simplify the problem

_____ Find a pattern             _____ Act it out                       _____ Write an equation

**Enrichment Options**

Create story problems for the class to do                                          _____ _____ _____ _____ _____

Choose a method from the top of the contract;
create 4-6 problems at different levels of difficulty                              _____ _____ _____ _____ _____

Study a math textbook from a higher grade level that
is different from the adopted text; find and record
problems that require specific problem-solving methods;
name the methods                                                                   _____ _____ _____ _____ _____

Select a problem that our school is experiencing;
apply several of the methods listed above to solve it                              _____ _____ _____ _____ _____

Apply several of the methods to solve a personal problem                           _____ _____ _____ _____ _____

Help another student to understand a problem-solving method                        _____ _____ _____ _____ _____

Create an activity related to problem-solving                                      _____ _____ _____ _____ _____

Teacher's signature _____      Student's signature _____

## HOW TO USE THE CONTRACT WITH PROBLEM-SOLVING FOCUS

1. Find or design an assessment tool or pretest for each problem-solving strategy. Offer the pretest before you teach each strategy, or when you observe that certain students have mastered a particular strategy.

2. On the top part of the contract, record the dates when the student masters specific strategies.

3. Create enrichment options, or use those shown on the sample contract.

   - Students write the date(s) on which they work on certain activities.

   - Each line provides time for a student to work on that task for one day.

- When all lines are used up, students should select other tasks, unless they are involved in a long-term activity which requires more time.

### CAUTION

Students' grades should come from the top part of the contract representing grade level work. You may choose to give some extra credit for enrichment options, if the students insist, but this should *never* be "extra credit" in addition to completed regular work. It should be "instead of" credit to replace easier activities on concepts students have already mastered.

## CONTRACT FOR READING SKILLS/GRAMMAR/LANGUAGE MECHANICS

Student's Name: _Leandra_ _____

_____ 58 (plurals)                _____ 62 (compound words)      _____ 65 (possessives)

_____ 59 (subject/verb agreement) _____ 63 (suffixes)           _____ 66 (possessives)

_____ 60 (prefixes)               _____ 64 (suffixes)           _____ 67 (parts of speech)

_____ 61 (prefixes)

### Alternate Activities

Record the way you spent your time while the rest of the class was working on concepts you have mastered. The only expectation is that you spend your time reading and/or writing.

| DATE | ACTIVITY |
|------|----------|
|      |          |
|      |          |
|      |          |
|      |          |

Teacher's signature _____   Student's signature _____

# HOW TO USE THE CONTRACT FOR READING SKILLS/GRAMMAR/LANGUAGE MECHANICS

1. On the top part of the contract, list required skills or textbook pages. The example shows both to illustrate your options.

2. To determine which concepts students have already mastered, allow them to take a pretest or to complete a product that demonstrates their competency.

3. Give contracts to those students who achieve a "B" or higher on the pretest, or demonstrate their competency by completing a product. Check only those skills they haven't yet learned, or pages that teach concepts they haven't mastered.

4. For a whole language program, use concepts instead of page numbers at the top of the contract. See Chapter 7 for other ideas.

### NOTE

Students on contract must attend the instructional lesson only when you are teaching the skills, pages, or concepts you have checked. On other days, they may read or write, keeping track of their activities on the spaces provided at the bottom of the contract.

# WORKING CONDITIONS FOR ALTERNATE ACTIVITIES

If you are working on alternate activities while others in the class are busy with more teacher-directed activities, you are expected to follow these guidelines:

1. Stay on task at all times with the alternate activities you have chosen.

2. Don't talk to the teacher while he or she is teaching.

3. When you need help, and the teacher is busy, ask someone else who is also working on the alternate activities.

4. If no one else can help you, continue to try the activity yourself until the teacher is available, or move on to another activity until the teacher is free.

5. Use "6-inch voices" when talking to each other about the alternate activities. (These are voices that can be heard no more than 6 inches away.)

6. Never brag about your opportunities to work on the alternate activities.

7. If you must go in and out of the room, do so soundlessly.

8. If you are going to work in another location, stay on task there, and follow the directions of the adult in charge.

9. Don't bother anyone else.

10. Don't call attention to yourself.

*I agree to the conditions described above, and know that if I don't follow them, I may lose the opportunity to continue with the alternate activities and may have to rejoin the class for teacher-directed instruction.*

Teacher's signature _____

Student's signature _____

learning contracts. You would keep their completed contracts in their compacting folders, along with all tests, as evidence of the alternate work they have done. Or, if you would like to include learning contract information on your Compactor, an example of how to do this is found on page 34.

### "How can I figure out the grades for students who do less work from the text than others?"

By averaging their scores, the same as for any other student. The difference is that these students will have *fewer* scores to average, since some of their time will have been spent on alternate activities.

In some cases, the students will earn grades for the alternate work they do, as explained in Chapter 8. These grades should never be lower than the grade the student would have earned if she had decided to work with the entire class instead of independently. Some teachers give students "credit" for following the working conditions of their contract.

### "How can I use the contract if I'm teaching whole language or other holistic thematic units?"

Using an adaptation of the learning contract on page 24, simply write in the learning outcomes instead of the pages or concepts.

*Example:* For a unit on Antarctica, the outcomes might be:

- Describe iceberg composition and dangers.

- Understand components of scientific expeditions.

- Create journal entries for an Antarctic explorer.

- Read several fiction and non-fiction books on the topic of Antarctica.

- Compute the math related to Antarctic scientific experiments.

Then create a menu of alternate activities from which students may chose *as soon as* they demonstrate mastery of the essential content.

As always, allow them to create an option of their choice.

### "What will I do when some students who could qualify for a contract choose not to take the pretest and indicate they would rather work with the class?"

Recall that many gifted students equate being gifted with getting their work done quickly. In their minds, someone who struggles must be less intelligent than someone who breezes through assignments. Why would they want to do the exciting (and challenging) activities you have designed for them? They can see that these activities will take more time.

Make it clear that their enrichment work will not be averaged in with their grade level work. If you do grade these activities, it won't take your students long to figure out that the contract option could jeopardize their grade. Why should they take such a risk? Instead, they'll choose to do what everyone else is doing.

Sometimes that behavior reflects a bid for social acceptance. Sometimes it's a way of playing it safe. If they take a risk—if they choose to struggle—they might fail. And if they fail, this will "prove" that they aren't really smart after all. It takes more intelligence to hang in there when the going gets tough than it does to excel in the "easy" work. This is what you must communicate to your gifted students.

### "Some students seem unwilling to work without close direction from me. How can I give them the time they need without taking time away from the other students?"

Gifted students need and want quality time with the teacher. Rather than teaching them directly all the time, it's up to you to take a more facilitative and guiding role. You will all enjoy time spent exploring alternate problem-solving strategies and learning how to use enrichment materials. It's also a good idea to allow students to work together on enrichment activities so they can help each other.

*"Shouldn't my gifted students be spending some of their time tutoring students who are having trouble learning?"*

ALL students in your class have the right to learn something new in your class every day, including your most capable students. Although there may be some benefits for all students when gifted students interact in a teaching capacity with those who need help, the practice of *consistently* having gifted students teach struggling students robs the gifted students of their right to struggle and learn. Your capable students might conclude, "Everyone else comes to school to learn math. Not me; I come to teach it." Or, "Once I've finished the material in the book, I've finished the subject, since the teacher never provides other types of activities for me."

You may find it much more effective to ask your "second layer" of excellent students to tutor those in need. These "teachers" will gain a better understanding of the concepts, and they may be more patient with those they are teaching. Gifted students can become very frustrated at always being asked to tutor, and the students they are

tutoring may say they understand a concept long before they do, just to escape from an uncomfortable situation. This issue is addressed in more detail in Chapter 9.

*"We don't use a textbook, except as a reference. We usually spend the entire math class on problem-solving experiences. Do my gifted students still need a differentiated program?"*

As instruction in mathematics moves away from an emphasis on computation to an emphasis on problem-solving for all students, differentiated math programming may not be as necessary for gifted students in the regular classroom. Are your gifted students being adequately challenged in math? Find out by observing their learning behavior. If they seem to be going through the motions, or if they refuse to do their work, they probably need alternate learning experiences. If they are actively engaged in learning and appear to be struggling to learn for much of the time, the activities you are already using may be adequate and need no enrichment. See page 30 for a way to use a contract approach in this type of math program.

---

## THE COMPACTOR
### Joseph Renzulli & Linda H. Smith

**Student's Name:** *Julie*

| Areas of Strength | Documenting Mastery | Alternate Activities |
|---|---|---|
| *Math Chapter 5* | *Score of 85 percent or higher on chapter pretest* | *Will work with class on days they learn concepts she has not mastered.*<br><br>*Will work on alternate activities on other days in enrichment center.* |
| *Math Chapter 6* | *Same as above* | *Same as above.* |
| | | |
| | | |

# SUMMARY

This chapter presents a learning contract system that is virtually guaranteed to work. The major difference between this system and others you may have used in the past is that students on contract are not allowed to race through the grade level assignments. Instead, they are required to wait to do them at the same time as the teacher is instructing the rest of the class on those topics. The contract students must also follow specific working conditions to remain eligible for contract status.

Contracts may be used in math, language arts, reading skill work, vocabulary, penmanship, and in all drill-and-practice situations. They may be adapted to science and social studies by listing concepts instead of pages on the top of the contract. Chapter 4 describes other methods to use with subjects that may not lend themselves to a traditional contract system.

Sometimes we teachers can force our students to do work they know they don't need, but they can make us wish we hadn't forced them. They respond with sloppy, careless, or messy work, turned in late or not at all. We fight back, sending notes home on a regular basis, but it's a losing battle. If you've been looking for a better way to motivate your students, try the learning contract system described in this chapter. You will need to do some preparation, but once the system is in place, it will practically run itself. Your reward will come as you watch your students perk up and willingly engage in challenging work. With this system, everybody wins.

## MORE RESOURCES FOR TEACHERS

- Galbraith, Judy. *The Gifted Kids Survival Guide (For Ages 10 & Under)*. Minneapolis, MN: Free Spirit Publishing Inc., 1984.

- Galbraith, Judy, and James Delisle. *The Gifted Kids Survival Guide: A Teen Handbook*, Revised and Updated Edition. Minneapolis, MN: Free Spirit Publishing Inc., 1996.

  Two guides to help gifted kids cope with the stresses, demands, and benefits that come with being gifted.

- Hegeman, Kathryn. *Gifted Children in the Regular Classroom*. Monroe, NY: Trillium Press, 1987.

  Identification and programming for all types of gifted students.

# COMPACTING THE CURRICULUM FOR LITERATURE, SCIENCE, AND SOCIAL STUDIES

The pretesting option only works if students have previously learned the curriculum. Other compacting methods are needed for what I call "Boring B" situations, in which the curriculum may be new, but gifted students can learn it much more quickly than their age peers.

For example, most of the curriculum in literature, science, and social studies is new each year. Therefore, it may not be appropriate for gifted students to say, "I have already learned this and that's why I'm bored" (the "Boring A" situation). Nevertheless, their attitude and behavior may communicate that they don't *want* to learn. Gifted students need to know how to express their frustration in "Boring B" situations. I teach my students to say, "At the present moment in time, I do not know enough about this topic to be interested in it." This usually brings a smile as students realize that they have offered an opinion based on no data!

One thing that truly separates gifted students at any grade level from their age peers is their ability to learn new material much more quickly and to a much greater depth of understanding. Yet they are often asked to first complete the "regular work" at the same pace as everyone else, after which they are offered some kind of "extra credit" project. No wonder they quickly conclude that this is no great honor. Why should they work twice as hard or long as the other students? Their problem isn't that they are bored with the *content* of the material. They are impatient with the *pace*. And the choice usually offered to them—more "extra credit" work—is not attractive.

This chapter describes strategies you can use to compact and differentiate the curriculum for gifted students in literature, science, and social studies—subjects that don't lend themselves to pretesting because the information has not been previously learned. To compact in these subjects means to reduce the amount of time gifted students must spend on grade level work. To differentiate in these subjects means that gifted students work on different activities than the rest of the class—alternate activities which allow them to explore topics in greater depth.

The strategies presented here are designed for teachers who use the textbook as an important part of their instruction. They also work for teachers who use the text as a guide but include many alternate activities. If you are a teacher who rarely uses the text, the strategies presented in Chapter 5 may be more appropriate for you.

# SCENARIO: JOEY

Joey, a student in my fifth-grade class, was gifted "across the board." His ability was exceptional in every subject area, as well as art and physical education. However, his actual classroom performance left a lot to be desired. I found it frustrating that he seemed to spend much of his class time daydreaming, and he seldom completed his homework assignments, but he *always* aced the tests! This happened even in social studies, where all of the material was supposed to be completely new. Furthermore, Joey behaved rudely during class discussions. He blurted out answers even when he wasn't called on, and he seemed to delight in making remarks under his breath that were designed to amuse and distract the other students.

I recognized that Joey's negative behavior was related to his superior learning ability. Rather than "disciplining" him, I decided to find a management system that would allow Joey to learn social studies in a manner more commensurate with his ability. Naturally, I hoped that the added challenge would have a positive effect on Joey's behavior, which frequently happens with gifted students.

# STRATEGY: THE STUDY GUIDE

When Joey's class was about to begin a four-week unit on the Civil War, I prepared the study guide shown on page 39. It covered the most important concepts in the text—those I wanted all of my students to master. All students would be tested *only* on the concepts covered in the study guide. Those students who qualified (as determined by me, not a pretest score) would be allowed time away from the class, when I was guiding the rest of the students through the text, to gather information about a related topic. They would be called "resident experts," and they would be responsible for presenting some kind of report about their topic to the class at an appropriate time.

This independent study method departs from the options described in earlier chapters in that it is *not* immediately offered to all students. As I explained to my class, it would be available only to those students who had demonstrated that they didn't need teacher direction to understand the textbook portion of a unit of study. However, I also reassured the class that everyone would have

a chance to become a resident expert at some time. This opportunity is described on pages 43 and 45.

I chose as many students as I believed could learn the textbook portion without my direction. Then I gathered the eligible students together and said:

"You know, there is a lot more to the Civil War than is included in our book. Although the rest of the class will be studying the textbook portion of this unit with me, my hunch is that you could probably get the information in the book simply by reading it on your own. If that's the case, I would be delighted if each of you would help me teach the Civil War by becoming resident experts on topics related to that conflict.

"I've prepared a study guide you can use to help you notice and learn what I consider to be the most important elements in the textbook. All you have to do is make sure that you learn the concepts listed on the study guide, and you may do this in school or at home. During the time the rest of the class is studying the book with me, you will be preparing a project—*not* a written report—which you will then share with the class to make this unit much more exciting and interesting for all of us. All of the work on your project will be done in school, so you have work to do during social studies time that may be more interesting to you than the text. You may work on your project in class, in the library, or in the learning center, but you may not take it home until it has been completed and shared with the class.

"Please read through the list of alternate topics I've prepared and see if you can find something there that interests you. Or perhaps you have an original idea. The only condition is that your topic must be related to the Civil War era. Next, you must decide what kind of project you will do. A list describing various types of acceptable projects is available for your use. You may also suggest a project that is not on the list."*

---

*I encourage you to send for a catalog from Creative Learning Press called "The Best of Methodological Resource Books." It lists and describes books that help young researchers emulate professionals in the physical and social sciences, mathematics and statistics, cartooning, public speaking, radio and television production, and many other fields of endeavor. Access to these books will provide students with other ideas for projects. See Appendix C, page 151.

## CIVIL WAR STUDY GUIDE

### Be prepared to:

1. Discuss the causes of the war.

2. Describe the basis of the economy for the North and the South.

   ★ **Quiz for 1 and 2 by January 19th** ★

3. Know the meaning of the vocabulary words listed on pages 89, 96, 104, and 115.

4. Complete a map of the states in 1861 to show which states seceded to the Confederacy and which stayed in the Union.

5. Recite from memory Lincoln's "Gettysburg Address."

   ★ **Quiz for 1-5 by February 1st** ★

6. Describe typical battle conditions which a soldier would be likely to encounter.

7. Narrate a 3-minute biographical sketch of any Civil War personality.

   ★ **Test for 1-7 by February 15th** ★

# HOW TO USE THE STUDY GUIDE

1. Select major concepts for the unit. Choose only those that are important enough to be evaluated.

2. Create a study guide activity for each major concept. List them in the general order in which they will be taught.

3. Indicate a timetable for assessing student progress. Inform students of when quizzes or discussions will be held. Let them know that they will be responsible at that time for all material taught up to that point.

4. Discuss alternate ways of learning textbook material. Let the students decide if they need to write out their answers.

5. Negotiate the terms of the Independent Study Contract (see the note below). Discuss them with the students. Have the students initial the conditions as they agree to them.

## NOTE

All students who use the study guide method must sign an Independent Study Contract, described on pages 42-43. If the terms of that contract are broken, the student rejoins the teacher-directed group.

A sample list of alternate Civil War topics is found below. A reproducible list of generic project ideas is found on page 41. Guidelines for developing alternate projects are provided in Chapter 6.

Why shouldn't students prepare a written report for their project? Because most learning done by gifted students is stored in their minds, and they experience very little added benefit by writing it out formally. Furthermore, students may decide against participating in the resident expert opportunity if a written product is required.

To make sure that my students understood the study guide, I went on to explain, "You will have to learn concepts 1 and 2 before January 19th, when the whole class will take a quiz on them. That date is written right on your study guide. If you score a 'B' or higher on the quiz,

you may keep working on your resident expert project until the next quiz. As long as you keep earning a 'B' or higher on quizzes and tests, you may continue to work on your project."

Regular quizzes and/or discussions enable you to verify that your resident experts are keeping up with the textbook material, rather than leaving it all for the end of the unit and cramming to learn it. Tell your students that anytime resident experts cannot earn a "B" or higher on a quiz, or if they display problematic behavior, they will be asked to rejoin the class until the next quiz. If they achieve an acceptable grade on the next quiz, they may return to their project. If they have to leave their project to rejoin the class until the end of the chapter or unit, they will be expected to complete it when the rest of the class gets school time to become resident experts.

## ALTERNATE TOPICS FOR CIVIL WAR UNIT

- Present a biography of someone who was important during the Civil War period. This should take the form of a first-person interview, with you playing the part of the famous person, and a friend playing the part of the interviewing reporter. Dressing up as the famous person would add interest and excitement to your report.

- Research the music of both the Union and the Confederacy. Teach the class one song from each side. Be prepared to describe their similarities and differences. You might also discover how music has been used to motivate people and influence their feelings during other wars.

- Demonstrate the action during a famous battle. Be sure to include information about the tactics used by both sides.

- Prepare a first-person diary account of the time period from the point of view of:

  —a soldier

  —a general

  —a field hospital doctor

  —a nurse

  —a woman who stayed at home while her husband and sons went off to war

  —a famous personality.

- Discover the actual conditions of being a slave. Include information about:

  —daily life

  —food

  —shelter

  —family safety

  —religion

  —clothing

  —the differences between the life of a field slave and the life of a house slave

  —and so on.

# ACCEPTABLE STUDENT PROJECTS

## For primary students:

- Draw or trace pictures that represent learning onto transparencies. Narrate information to listeners as your pictures are shown.

- Use a graphic "map" or chart that the teacher has used in other settings. Examples: story map, character chart, advance organizer.

- Survey others; transfer your data to a chart or graph.

- Create a game for others to play to learn the same information.

- Create a mobile, diorama, display, or other visual representation of your data.

- Create dictionaries for specific topics, or translate words into another language.

- Draw attribute webs. Write brief topic ideas on the spokes of the web. Example:

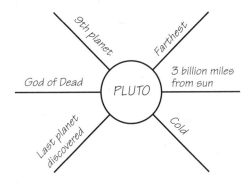

## For students in all other grades:

- Choose an idea from the primary section above.

- Make a filmstrip on blank filmstrip material; narrate.

- Create a puppet show and present it.

- Create a radio or television broadcast or a video production.

- Hold a panel discussion, round-robin discussion, or debate.

- Write a diary or journal of an important historical event or person; write a speech a person might have made at the time.

- Create a time line of events: personal, historical, social, etc.

- Working with several other students, create a panel discussion about a topic of a certain historical time period *or* about how different historical figures might react to a current problem of today.

- Create an invention to fill a personal or social need.

- Present biographical information dressed as the person investigated.

- Write a song, rap, poem, story, advertisement, or jingle.

- Create a travel brochure for another country or planet.

- Create an imaginary country from papier-mâché. Locate essential features.

- Make a model; describe its parts and the functions of each.

- Create a chart or poster to represent synthesis of information.

- Write a script for a play or a mock trial.

- Write a journal of time spent and activities completed with a mentor in the community.

- Collect materials from a lobbying or public service agency; summarize information. (TIP: Use the *Encyclopedia of Associations* found in the reference section of most public libraries.)

- Write to people in other places about specific topics; synthesize their responses.

- Create a learning center for teachers to use in their classrooms.

- Rewrite a story, setting it in another time period, after researching probable differences.

- Gather political cartoons from several sources; analyze the cartoonists' ideas.

- Critique a film, book, television show, or video program; write an editorial and send it to your local newspaper.

- Write a how-to manual for those who need instruction on how to do or use something.

- Contact publishers to find out how to get something you've written published.

- Come up with your own ideas.

Some teachers use class discussions instead of written quizzes. Resident experts are expected to participate in those discussions on the days indicated. Their level of participation indicates the degree to which they have mastered the concepts.

All work on the resident expert project is done in school, replacing the textbook portion of the instruction. Resident experts are not expected to write reports about what they have learned unless the whole class is required to write reports. Their work is judged on the *complexity and sophistication of content and thought processes* rather than appearance—on *substance* rather than form. For guidelines on how to evaluate resident expert projects, see pages 46-48.

Finally, each student must sign an Independent Study Contract describing what is expected of him or her during the unit of study. Students keep copies of their contract with their study guide so they can refer to it when necessary. The contract is described in the following section; you'll find a reproducible contract form on page 44.

# STRATEGY: THE INDEPENDENT STUDY CONTRACT

Any number of things could potentially go wrong with a resident expert arrangement to make it a less than satisfying experience for you and your students. The Independent Study Contract is designed to guard against misunderstandings, disagreements, and claims such as, "You never told me I had to pass any quizzes!"

All resident experts must enter into a contract with the teacher that describes the conditions of their independent study. Instructions for how to use the contract are found on page 45. Feel free to change any of these conditions or add new ones of your own. Then call a group meeting with your resident experts to introduce the contract. You might say, "Each of you is expected to sign a contract that explains my expectations for you while you are working as a resident expert. As you agree to each condition, please write your initials on the line to the left. Please keep your contract with your study guide at all time." For convenience, some teachers print the contract and study guide back-to-back on a single sheet of paper.

My private name for this document is the "Worst-Case Scenario Contract." It has been designed to prevent teachers from saying, "This

was a terrible mistake and I'm never going to do it again!" Here's how it works.

The first item states, "The student may learn the key concepts or the information described on the study guide independently." You may want to go through the study guide with the group, making sure everyone understands the vocabulary and expectations. Inevitably, someone will ask the question, "Do we have to write out the answers?" Your response might be, "Use whatever methods are necessary to make sure you learn the material. How you do it is up to you."

You might wonder, "How will I know the students are learning the material?" You probably won't know until you get to the quizzes or discussions, at which point it should become very clear. Meanwhile, how much "policing" will you need to do? None! If the resident experts fail to meet the conditions of the contract, the logical consequence is that they will have to spend their time with the rest of the class, being taught the material at a pace designed for the larger group. Students decide which method they prefer, and learn from experience what will happen if they don't follow the terms of the contract.

The second item on the contract states, "The student must demonstrate competency with any assessment activity, in order to continue this same arrangement for the rest of this unit." The score should be equivalent to a "B" or higher. This grade is not unreasonable, because the textbook material should be simple enough for these students to learn independently. Why not insist on an "A"? Because teachers need to demonstrate that students don't have to earn "A"'s to be considered gifted, and that even students who are considered gifted don't have to earn "A"'s all the time.*

The third item on the contract states, "The student must participate in selected group activities when one day's notice is given by the teacher." This requirement came out of an experience I had while trying out this method with a class during a unit on the Civil War. I was walking through the hall one day when my principal saw me and gave me one of those ghastly looks. "Oh, my gosh," she said. "I forgot to do your third observation this year. My deadline is next week. What are you doing tomorrow afternoon at 2:20?" She already knew what I was doing because she had my lesson plans. I had scheduled a discussion about the Civil War with the regu-

---

*Parents may not agree. For tips on winning support from parents, see Chapter 11, page 134.

lar class; the resident experts would be out working on their projects. A little voice inside me started shrieking, "If my resident experts aren't there, the quality of the discussion may leave much to be desired!" From that point on, my Independent Study Contract stipulated that resident experts would be present in class on one day's notice from me.

Being observed by the principal is just one reason why you might want your resident experts to attend class on a given day. As a creative teacher, you probably don't spend all of your class time using the textbook. You involve your students in many other interesting and stimulating activities, some of which everyone should be present for. You need to reserve the option of calling in your resident experts for these activities.

The fourth item on the contract states, "The student agrees to complete an independent project by _____(date) to share with the class." Emphasize that this project *will* be shared with the class. Students should keep this in mind as they decide what kind of project they will do. For students who resist making a "live" presentation, a video of their presentation may be substituted.

Next, the contract provides space for students to describe the project they have chosen. They might draw a diagram of it or describe it in words. This is your chance to check the appropriateness of each project. Basically, a resident expert project should be:

- broad enough to be relevant to the entire unit,

- involved enough to hold the student's interest for that period of time,

- sophisticated enough to provide a valid showcase for the student's talents,

- manageable enough to be completed by the end of the unit, and

- reflective of the student's ability to think in more abstract and complex ways than his or her age peers.

For example, our friend Joey was interested in trains, so he offered to draw the trains and locomotives of the Civil War period. However, simply drawing the trains would not have provided an adequate challenge to his superior learning ability. So we negotiated a project that allowed Joey to draw his trains on a huge piece of tagboard on which he also located the major Civil War battlefields and manufacturing centers. Joey's second task was to determine the extent to which the proximity of the manufacturing centers to the bat-

tlefields affected the outcome of the war. His contract, shown on page 46, represents a legitimate "gifted activity." It forced Joey to become more original with his thinking, and to synthesize information from many sources to create and defend a hypothesis.

The blank lines at the bottom of the contract are for you to fill in with whatever you think needs to be there, including anything you suspect will drive you crazy if it isn't stipulated at the outset. For example, you might write, "Students agree to enter and leave the room soundlessly, without calling any undue attention to themselves." Since it is unlikely that you will continue to offer independent study opportunities that make you feel frustrated or uncomfortable, you should include any conditions you believe will make this system work. See the form in Chapter 3, page 32 for suggestions and ideas.

You should continue to meet with your resident expert group on a regular basis to provide technical assistance for their projects, and to give those students their fair share of your time and attention.

## QUESTIONS AND ANSWERS ABOUT INDEPENDENT STUDY

*"Isn't it possible that other students will want to become resident experts, too?"*

Of course it's possible. There are at least two ways you can handle this situation. You might offer a culminating activity in which you list all of the topics that are covered in the unit, and ask for students to volunteer to work alone or in groups to gather additional information beyond what's in the textbook. Then each student or group could make an informal report to the class about what they have discovered. The original resident experts could use this time to complete any unfinished projects. Again, students should *not* have to prepare a formal written report. Their presentation should include some kind of visual aid illustrating what the students want the rest of the class to understand about their information.

A second way to involve the rest of the students as resident experts was developed by a seventh-grade science teacher, who was so pleased with the results that he decided to adapt the model for use with all of his students. Using a unit on basic chemistry, the teacher began by giving his class a global overview of the chapter contents, reasoning that it

# INDEPENDENT STUDY CONTRACT

The following terms are agreed to by teacher and student:

_____ The student may learn the key concepts or the information described on the study guide independently.

_____ The student must demonstrate competency with any assessment activity, in order to continue this same arrangement for the rest of this unit.

_____ The student must participate in selected group activities when one day's notice is given by the teacher.

_____ The student agrees to complete an independent project by _____(date) to share with the class.

A description of the project follows:

_____

_____

_____

_____

The student agrees to work on the selected project according to the following guidelines while the remainder of the class is involved with the teacher.

_____

_____

_____

Teacher's signature _____

Student's signature _____

would be very difficult for students to understand how to become an expert on a small piece of the unit if they didn't get the big picture first.* Students then chose their topics, and the teacher allowed two to three days of in-class time for information gathering. Meanwhile, he brought in special materials from sources other than the textbook for the students to use as needed. He listed the topics on butcher paper while the students were doing their research, so everyone could see clearly which topics came before and after their own.

Instead of lecturing or doing a round-robin reading of the textbook material, the teacher launched the actual study of the unit by saying, "The first topic we will consider is the atom, and

our resident expert, Janice, will tell us about it." Janice came forward and shared what she had learned about atoms. When she was finished, the teacher asked the rest of the class if anyone had anything to add. He invented an ingenious rule for this stage of the game: "Anyone who repeats something the expert already said won't be called on for the rest of the discussion." This is the kind of challenge gifted students enjoy, because 1) they must listen so they're sure not to add something that's already been said, and 2) they have more opportunities to contribute, since they *always* have something to add! This is all part of what it means to be gifted: learning and remembering so much, and taking such pleasure in letting the world know how much you know.

After giving the students a chance to speak, the teacher added any information he thought had been overlooked. Then he moved on to the next topic by asking, "Who is our resident expert on molecules?" As subsequent resident experts described what they had learned, they were required to state, sometime during the first 30 seconds of their talk, how their topic was related to the previous topic. This encouraged students to listen to the other presentations, and to think about connections as they learned the material.

Thanks to his inventiveness, this teacher made an important discovery: *All* of his students appeared to learn more with this method than with the traditional methods he had been using. They became more excited about the topics, and their motivation to learn was significantly higher. This is an excellent example of how strategies brought into the classroom to benefit gifted students can have serendipitous spillover effects with other students as well.

*"What happens if the resident experts don't finish their projects?"*

The logical consequence is that they won't be eligible to work independently for the following unit. The same consequence applies if they disrupt the class or fail to meet other conditions of the contract. If you create resident expert opportunities for the entire class as a culminating activity, those students who didn't finish their projects would be expected to complete them at this time.

---

## HOW TO USE THE INDEPENDENT STUDY CONTRACT

1. Meet with all students who will become resident experts.

2. Describe all terms and conditions on the contract. Students initial each one to indicate their understanding and agreement.

3. Invite students to describe their project in the space provided. The project should be appropriately complex, and it should not take the form of a written report.

4. Agree on the evaluation expectations.
   • Differentiate between the type of work necessary for an "A" and a "B."
   • Tell students that they select their desired grade by the type of project they choose.

   See pages 46-48 for guidelines on how to evaluate resident expert projects.

5. Meet regularly with the resident experts.
   • Ask them to report on their progress.
   • Help them to locate resources.
   • Encourage them to persist even when frustrated.

6. Provide regular class time for resident experts to share their projects with the entire class or an appropriate audience.

---

*Some ways to present a global overview include showing a film or video, surveying the unit visually and predicting upcoming content, and having students read any questions they will be expected to answer at a later time.

*"How can I make sure that a student's parents don't get involved in trying to influence the content or quality of the resident expert project?"*

Easy: The project doesn't go home until it is completed! It is designed to be done in school so more capable students have meaningful work to do while the rest of the class is learning the basics with the teacher. The project represents the student's "real work" in school, and it must be available in school whenever it is needed. This includes work on any visual aid. Interested parents can assist their resident experts by helping them to locate information, or by taking them to museums and other sources of information.

*"How should I evaluate resident expert projects?"*

One way is to simply average the actual grades the students earn, even if some students earn fewer grades than others. The rationale for this is discussed in Chapter 3, page 33. However, most teachers and students feel the need to connect a

---

## INDEPENDENT STUDY CONTRACT

The following terms are agreed to by teacher and student:

_J.N._   The student may learn the key concepts or the information described on the study guide independently.

_J.N._   The student must demonstrate competency with any assessment activity, in order to continue this same arrangement for the rest of this unit.

_J.N._   The student must participate in selected group activities when one day's notice is given by the teacher.

_J.N._   The student agrees to complete an independent project by ___December 15___ (date) to share with the class.

A description of the project follows:

*Show how distances between battlefields and factories affected the outcome of the Civil*

*War. Draw trains and battlefields on 24" x 36" poster board.*

_____

_____

The student agrees to work on the selected project according to the following guidelines while the remainder of the class is involved with the teacher.

*All those above*

*Joey will not brag about his work on his project*

*Joey will keep his project at school*

Teacher's signature     *Joey Nelson*

Student's signature     *Mrs. Winebrenner*

grade to the resident expert project. The Independent Study Project Evaluation Contract on page 48 is one way to design an equitable grading system. Students who work on independent study should be guaranteed an "A" or a "B," since they have chosen to work with advanced material. The difference between those two grades is that a project earns a "B" if the student collects data others have found. The project earns an "A" if the student does original research.

A contract I designed especially for Joey is shown below. With everything spelled out in the beginning, Joey knew exactly what grade his work would earn. Feel free to add your own expectations about the quality of the projects you would like your students to produce. Or you might ask your students to describe their project ideas, then offer some suggestions as to grade considerations.

## EVALUATION CONTRACT

### Civil War Project

**For a grade of "B," use information gathered from other sources.**

Choose from the ideas below, or design your own with my approval:

1. Research the different types of trains and locomotives that would have been used during the Civil War era. Draw them to scale.

2. Discover the details about the lives of two famous generals, one Union and one Confederate. Comment on at least two similarities you find.

3. Learn several Civil War songs from both sides. Teach one song from each side to the class. Lead the class in a discussion of similarities and differences in the songs.

**For a grade of "A," create a unique product that requires high levels of thinking.**

Choose from the ideas below, or design your own with my approval:

1. Draw the trains of the Civil War era on routes between the major manufacturing centers and four famous battlefields: two in the North and two in the South. Be prepared to discuss how the proximity of the battlefields to the manufacturing centers may have affected the outcome of the war.

2. Create an interview with a famous Civil War general. Include some information that was probably unknown to the general public at the time of the Civil War. Prepare a live interview where you and a friend impersonate the general and the interviewer. Come in appropriate costume.

3. Discover the role that music has played to create and maintain patriotic feelings during wartime. Illustrate your presentation with musical excerpts.

Use this space to describe your project:

*Do #1.*

I am contracting for a grade of ___*A*___.

Student's signature ___*Joey Nelson*___

# INDEPENDENT STUDY PROJECT EVALUATION CONTRACT

### For a grade of "B":

**1.** Use secondary sources to prepare your project.

**2.** Use a standard format.

### For a grade of "A":

**1.** Use primary sources (interviews, surveys, diaries, journals, etc.).

**2.** Really "get into" your topic.  Produce a "real-life" product.

**3.** Present your information to an appropriate audience.

**4.** Use a unique presentation format.  Ideas: Appear as your subject. Create an original filmstrip, video, etc.

Use this space to describe your project:

_____

_____

_____

_____

_____

_____

Teacher's signature _____

Student's signature _____

# SUMMARY

This chapter describes how to set up independent study projects for gifted students. The students become "resident experts" on topics related to the regular curriculum by learning new material from a more challenging perspective. Methods to manage those independent studies are presented, giving you specific, classroom-tested ways to compact and differentiate instruction for students in subject areas that may not lend themselves to pretesting. Some teachers still provide pretesting opportunities in these subjects and use the learning contracts approach described in Chapter 3 to manage the alternate activities for students who pass the pretest. Some teachers pretest and use the Independent Study Contract on page 44 to manage the students' alternate activities. The choice is yours.

# MORE RESOURCES FOR TEACHERS

- Feldhusen, Hazel. *Individualized Teaching of Gifted Children in Regular Classrooms.* East Aurora, NY: D.O.K. Publishers, 1986.

  Mini-lessons for teachers about all aspects of providing for the learning needs of gifted students in regular classrooms.

- Grun, Bernard. *Timetables of History: Horizontal Linkage of People and Events.* New Third Revised Edition. New York: Touchstone Books, 1991.

  Full-page charts illustrate what was happening in all parts of the world during a given time span in history.

# "I'M DONE. NOW WHAT SHOULD I DO?"

It's always a possibility that gifted students will finish an activity before the rest of the group. This produces considerable anxiety in classroom teachers, who typically respond by suggesting "extra credit" work. What prevents most teachers from offering appropriate alternatives is the specter of kids with time on their hands, nagging them for things to do. In fact, most gifted kids don't need to be spoon-fed activities to keep them busy. They just want some time to do things that are interesting to them without having to account for their work in a formal sense.

If we recall when "time on task" was considered to be a foolproof way to guarantee learning, we can understand why we feel reluctant to give our students "free time." When we speak of whether a student is "using her time wisely," we usually mean that she should look busy. She should be reading something, writing something, or doing something else observable to indicate that she is staying on task.

If you tried the Most Difficult First strategy described in Chapter 1, you discovered how easy it is to allow some students to do whatever they want with the time they buy. Some kids like to read. Others may be in the middle of writing stories and will eagerly return to them. Some may use their time to daydream, which is essential to problem-solving and creative thinking. Others may be curious about a topic or idea and would love to spend some school time exploring it. Gifted students tend to get passionately interested in topics that are not connected with the curriculum, and that is one reason why school is so inadequate for them. They are usually not given opportunities to learn the things they want to learn. Even when they are, those opportunities may not be very satisfying. The teacher says, "Well, do a report on it"—with the underlying message, "Make sure it's done well and looks good." But doing a report just means working harder than everybody else. Why would any student want to do that?

Furthermore, teachers worry that students will choose topics that are too broad, so we steer them toward narrower topics—those that can be turned into good reports. Given how rapidly information is growing and changing, we should be encouraging gifted students to explore a topic in depth before requiring formal feedback on a small part of it. This chapter presents several ways of dealing with students who need more than the regular curriculum provides. These strategies may also be used by those of you who teach with thematic units, and who thought that the strategies described in chapters 3 and 4 may not be applicable to your teaching style. Even in whole language classrooms, certain students will need the opportunities for independent study described here.

# SCENARIO: MARY JO

Mary Jo entered second grade reading at a sixth-grade level. She was comfortable with math concepts at about the third-grade level. She was placed in a third-grade room for reading and math, but stayed with her second-grade peers for all other subjects and activities. She also read five to eight books a day, which she kept hidden in her desk.

Her teacher was frustrated. She encouraged Mary Jo to spend time reading, hoping that the child would discover a topic she would want to pursue in some depth. But Mary Jo seemed content to do the same second-grade seatwork the other students were doing, even though she had clearly mastered the concepts they covered.

One day in early October, the teacher kept Mary Jo in from recess and took her to the school library. They were browsing when Mary Jo noticed a book about ancient Rome on display, and asked why it was being featured. The teacher said the most important words any teacher can say when working with gifted students: "I don't know, but I can probably help you find out." The bookmark indicated a section on how the ancient Roman celebration of the harvest festival contributed to the American celebration of Thanksgiving. Mary Jo was enthusiastically interested. "Were there any other ancient civilizations that had similar customs?" she wanted to know. "Let's find out," the teacher suggested.

Twenty minutes later, Mary Jo left the library with six books, each on a different ancient civilization. She also had six blank transparency sheets and, since she believed she could not draw well, a quick lesson in how to use the opaque projector to copy pictures from books. Her task was to browse through each book, one at a time, for as long as she liked. She was also free to locate other resources by herself or with her parents' help. When she had thoroughly researched the Roman harvest festival, she was to find a picture representing that celebration, transfer it to a blank transparency, color it, and give it to the teacher for

safekeeping. She would then go on to explore another civilization in the same manner, looking for information on harvest festivals and preparing a picture. At the end of her project, she would give a "transparency talk" to the class, showing her pictures and telling what she had learned.

During the next several weeks, Mary Jo became so interested in her project that she chose to do almost none of the regular second-grade work. Instead, she continued to read about ancient civilizations—*without taking notes*. Her teacher watched, amazed, as Mary Jo simply synthesized what she had read into the pictures she created on the transparencies. On the day of her talk, Mary Jo used the overhead projector to share with her classmates what she had learned. Unfortunately, the teacher had forgotten to set a time limit, so Mary Jo went on for *42 minutes* about how the people in six ancient civilizations celebrated their harvest festivals. Although her classmates were courteous, they nearly knocked out a wall getting out to recess when her report was over.

Remember that the child had taken no notes. She had kept all of the information in her head. That's part of what being gifted is all about: possessing abilities to think and remember that exceed those of one's age peers.

The teacher kept track of Mary Jo's skills and projects with a Compactor, as described in Chapter 2. Mary Jo's Compactor is found on page 53.

# STRATEGY FOR THE PRIMARY GRADES: INDEPENDENT STUDY WITH VISUAL AIDS

For gifted students in the primary grades, independent study projects may be relatively unstructured. It's important for them to have the chance to work on long-term, ongoing projects, returning to them whenever they have the time. Independent study with visual aids is a developmentally appropriate way for primary students to explore their areas of interest.

Students enjoy this strategy because they are allowed to investigate large amounts of information without immediately having to report on everything they read; most are willing to create more formal projects on individual subtopics later, when they have had the chance to satisfy their curiosity. The expectation that visual aids will be included in the presentation relieves them of the burden of doing too much writing.  Teachers enjoy this strategy because the projects remain the same for several days or weeks, and they are relieved of the responsibility for providing numerous shorter activities for those students who always seem to complete their regular work quickly.

No special forms are required to implement this strategy with primary students.  The teacher and student simply agree on a method the student will use to share the information with the class.  The "transparency talk" Mary Jo presented is one example.  For additional suggestions, see Acceptable Student Projects on page 41 of Chapter 4.

# SCENARIO: JASON

By the end of the first day of school, Jason was "done" with sixth grade.  It was painfully clear to his teacher that there was little or nothing in the assigned curriculum that represented new learning for Jason.  Worse still, his class had more than its share of struggling students.  No wonder his constant refrain was, "I'm done!  Now what should I do?"

Although Jason was obviously precocious, his parents did not want him to be promoted to a higher grade.  Therefore, it was necessary for the teacher to find an interesting, ongoing task that would keep him busy and learning without creating extra work for her.  She took Jason aside one day and said, "I've observed that you're frequently finished with your work very quickly, and you have a lot of time on your hands.  Would you like to use some of that time to investigate a topic that is of interest to you?  What might that be?"  Jason's instant response was, "Antarctica."  The teacher said, "Sounds like an interesting topic!  Let's see what resources we can find."

The teacher contacted the school librarian, who started to gather information from many different sources.*  When Jason visited the library, he came back loaded down with books, pamphlets, filmstrips, and magazines.  The teacher provided a place in the classroom for Jason to store his

---

*If your school does not have enough resources available, contact your public librarians.  These professionals are usually very happy to help you collect resources on a specific topic, and to arrange for an extended loan of up to six weeks.

---

## THE COMPACTOR
### Joseph Renzulli & Linda H. Smith

**Student's Name:**  _Mary Jo_

| Areas of Strength | Documenting Mastery | Alternate Activities |
|---|---|---|
| Reading | Passed end-of-book test for second-grade book | Placed in third-grade group for reading |
| Math | Passed end-of-book test for second-grade book | Placed in third-grade group for math |
| Second-grade seatwork | Advanced abilities and placement in reading and math<br><br>Superior writing ability—stories collected in portfolio | Resident expert on harvest festivals of ancient civilizations<br><br>Presented "transparency talk" to classmates |
|  |  |  |

materials. Whenever he had time left over after finishing his compacted work, he could go to "his shelf" and retrieve something to browse through.

At the start of the project, Jason had asked the teacher, "How much work" (meaning writing) "will I have to do?" She had said, "You may use the first several weeks to explore your topic before you start taking notes or worrying about a formal project." Relieved, he became thoroughly engrossed in learning about Antarctica.

# STRATEGY: INDEPENDENT STUDY USING THE TOPIC BROWSING PLANNER AND THE RESIDENT EXPERT PLANNER

Many teachers have given students the impression that all reading done in school must be "for a reason" and must result in a formal product, usually a report. However, we adults frequently enter bookstores or other people's homes and browse through books, idly wondering if we would like to know more about a certain topic at a later time. We would be offended if a bookstore owner posted a sign proclaiming, "NO BROWSING ALLOWED!" Why not provide opportunities for students to browse in school?

When we ask students to select a topic for a project, we usually insist that they do it quickly. Then we encourage them to narrow large topics down to smaller, more manageable subtopics. But how can students decide on smaller topics before they have a chance to explore the larger topic? Browsing lets them discover topics they never knew existed, any one of which may become the focus of their actual research.

The Topic Browsing Planner on page 55 creates opportunities for students to pursue topics that interest them. This work is done *in school, after* the students have completed their compacted work, and *instead of* the work the rest of the class is doing. Browsing time may be bought by demonstrating mastery of certain concepts on a pretest, by completing the Most Difficult First problems on an assignment, and/or by finishing compacted work assignments quickly and carefully.

The Planner may be used initially to provide some structure to a student's browsing, and later to help the student select a subtopic for more in-depth study. It helps students to keep track of

# HOW TO USE THE TOPIC BROWSING PLANNER

1. Help the student select a topic to investigate.

   Topics don't have to be related to the curriculum. Utilize the services of library personnel, both school and public.

2. Provide a place for the student to store accumulated resource materials.

   Suggestions: Space on a bookshelf; an empty desk.

3. Explain to the student how to fill out the Planner.

   During the exploration phase (5-10 days), students should fill in all sections except "How I Can Share What I've Learned." Remind them to take no formal notes during browsing time.

4. Meet with the student after the browsing is completed. Help the student to select a subtopic to research and present to the class.

   Encourage students to choose subtopics of genuine interest to them. If they don't wish to pursue any subtopic, allow them to move on to another topic. When they do choose a subtopic, help them to complete a Resident Expert Planner (page 59 or 60).

5. Make sure the student understands that he or she must choose one subtopic to study in depth for every three browsing experiences.

   If students resist, try to find out why. Perhaps they are reluctant to get up in front of the class for any reason; working together, you should be able to develop a mutually acceptable way for them to share their information.

# TOPIC BROWSING PLANNER

Student's name: _____ Date: _____

GENERAL TOPIC OF INTEREST: _____

SUBTOPICS I WANT TO LEARN MORE ABOUT (use the back for more ideas):

_____     _____

_____     _____

HOW I MIGHT COLLECT INFORMATION ABOUT THIS TOPIC:

| INFORMATION SOURCES | CALL NUMBER, AUTHOR, OR DATE | TITLE | WHERE I FOUND IT |
|---|---|---|---|
| Books: | | | |
| Periodicals: (magazines, newspapers, etc.) | | | |
| Other Sources: (TV, radio, etc.) | | | |

PROFESSIONALS WITH WHOM I MIGHT CONDUCT INTERVIEWS:

Name                          Profession              Workplace

_____

_____

_____

EXPERIMENTS OR SURVEYS I MIGHT CONDUCT: _____

_____

_____

HOW I CAN SHARE WHAT I'VE LEARNED ABOUT ONE SUBTOPIC: _____

_____

_____

any subtopics they may wish to explore, and it guides them in deciding how they will share what they have learned. You should anticipate using the Planner for each potential independent study. Tell your students at the outset that they are not to take any formal notes for a period of five to ten days. Instead, they are to use that time to browse through all the information they can find on their general topic of interest.

Jason's Planner, below, shows the results of three days' browsing of his topic, Antarctica.

When he discovered a subtopic he found interesting, he recorded it under "Subtopics I Want to Learn More About." "Information Sources" were listed by author, title, and library (school or public). Other potential sources of information, including periodicals and potential interview subjects, were noted in the appropriate spaces. For "Experiments and Surveys I Might Conduct," Jason wrote, "How the changing speed of melting ice affects stationary objects and land forms."

---

## TOPIC BROWSING PLANNER

**Student's name:** *Jason*                                                   **Date:** *October 5*

**GENERAL TOPIC OF INTEREST:** *Antarctica*

**SUBTOPICS I WANT TO LEARN MORE ABOUT:**

*Antarctic wildlife*             *Human survival in Antarctica*

*Fast melting of polar ice caps*       *Female Antarctic explorers*

**HOW I MIGHT COLLECT INFORMATION ABOUT THIS TOPIC:**

| INFORMATION SOURCES | CALL NUMBER, AUTHOR, OR DATE | TITLE | WHERE I FOUND IT |
|---|---|---|---|
| Books: | *Hackwell, W.J.* | *DESERT OF ICE* | *School Library* |
| | *Seth, Roland* | *ANTARCTICA* | *School Library* |
| | *Byrd, Richard* | *ANTARCTICA: Accounts...* | *Baxter Library* |
| Periodicals: (magazines, newspapers, etc.) | *February 1992 Shapiro, D.* *October 1989 Madson, M.* | *SAILING* "Letter from Antarctica" *WOMEN'S SPORTS* "The Last Continent" | |
| Other Sources: (TV, radio, etc.) | | | |

**PROFESSIONALS WITH WHOM I MIGHT CONDUCT INTERVIEWS:**

| Name | Profession | Workplace |
|---|---|---|
| *Dr. L.K. Olsen* | *Antarctic scholar* | *Shedd Aquarium, Chicago* |

**EXPERIMENTS OR SURVEYS I MIGHT CONDUCT:**

*How the changing speed of melting ice affects stationary objects and land forms*

**HOW I CAN SHARE WHAT I'VE LEARNED ABOUT ONE SUBTOPIC:**

*Biographies of 2 female explorers*

*Mock interviews*

At the end of his browsing time, Jason met with his teacher and was encouraged to create a more structured project about one subtopic to share with the class.  Delighted to learn that his project should not be a formal written report, he chose to create brief biographies of two female explorers, then present them to the class as mock interviews.  His choices are shown on his Planner under "How I Can Share What I've Learned about One Subtopic."  For additional project suggestions, see Acceptable Student Projects on page 41 of Chapter 4.

What if a student decides that he doesn't wish to pursue any subtopic in greater depth?  Simply file his Planner in the folder that contains his compacting records, and let him move on to something else.  Tell your students that you expect them to study one subtopic in depth for every three planners they complete.  For students who are too shy to present their projects to an audience, you might allow them to videotape their presentations, then play the video for the class.

Once a student chooses a subtopic to research, she has essentially agreed to become a "resident expert" and moves on to the next stage of the independent study.  An Upper Grades Resident Expert Planner is found on page 59.

# STRATEGY FOR THE PRIMARY GRADES: INDEPENDENT STUDY USING THE RESIDENT EXPERT PLANNER

Younger students also enjoy becoming resident experts.  They relish opportunities to pursue topics of their choosing in some detail.  Since their attention span is shorter than that of older students, and since fewer reference materials are available to them, I use a single form that combines the Topic Browsing Planner and the Resident Expert Planner.  It isn't nearly as detailed, and younger students find it manageable.  A Primary Grades Resident Expert Planner is found on page 60.

# STRATEGY FOR ALL GRADES: THE INTEREST SURVEY

What if a student needs a topic but can't think of one?  Here's where an Interest Survey can be very helpful.  You'll find a reproducible survey to use with your students on page 62.

Interest surveys allow you to learn things about your students that may not typically come to your attention.  You may wish to survey *all* of your students at the beginning of every school year.  Besides giving you insights into the kinds of things your gifted students may want to study in depth, the interest survey can also help you to motivate reluctant learners.  Raymond Wlodkowski, an educational psychologist and expert on motivation, has found that one of the quickest ways to motivate students is to discover what they are interested in outside of school, then spend a short time each day talking to them about their interests.  Watch for dramatic, positive changes in a relatively short period of time.

# STRATEGY: INDEPENDENT STUDY MENU

Just as children enjoy choosing their favorite foods from a restaurant menu, they like the fun and challenge of selecting activities from a "menu" of possibilities.  The Tic-Tac-Toe Menu on page 63 shows how this approach may be used to study a particular author.  The reproducible version that follows on page 64 is a generic model for managing a student's independent study.

The Tic-Tac-Toe aspect is optional; you may prefer your students to choose a certain number of activities without following any obvious pattern.  It's a good idea to set the criteria for evaluation *before* the student begins working on the activities.  See Chapter 8 for ways to evaluate the work of gifted students.

# HOW TO USE THE UPPER GRADES RESIDENT EXPERT PLANNER

1. Help the student select one subtopic from the Topic Browsing Planner.

   A subtopic should be something the student really wants to learn more about. Ask the student to make sure that there is sufficient information about his or her subtopic.

2. List the subtopic on the line, "The Subtopic I Will Study from the Topic Browsing Planner."

3. Direct the student to list specific things he or she wants to learn about the subtopic.

   Encourage students to choose items that reflect higher levels of thinking. (See Chapter 6, pages 67-69, for information on Bloom's Taxonomy.)

4. Direct the student to gather information from a variety of sources.

   Encourage students to use both school and public library facilities. Ask the librarians to help students explore technological sources.

5. Set a time limit for the student's report to the class, and direct the student to share only the sections he or she thinks other students will find most interesting.

   Don't limit the amount of data students gather—just the amount they present. Provide time and opportunities for students to share the balance of their data with other audiences including yourself, professionals in the field, librarians, etc.

6. Help the student choose a method for sharing the information.

   For ideas, see Acceptable Student Projects on page 41 of Chapter 4.

# UPPER GRADES RESIDENT EXPERT PLANNER

Student's name: _____ Date: _____

The Subtopic I Will Study from the Topic Browsing Planner:

_____

What I Want to Learn About: _____

_____

_____

_____

Sources of Information Used in My Study: _____

_____

_____

_____

The Most Interesting Information I Discovered: _____

_____

_____

_____

How I Will Share What I've Learned with an Audience: _____

_____

_____

_____

Date I Will Be Ready to Share Some Information: _____

# PLANNING THE GRADE YOU WILL EARN

Each activity has been assigned a certain number of points. To earn a certain final grade for your work in this unit, complete as many activities as needed to collect points for the grade you want.

- For a grade of "A," you must earn 45-50 points

- For a grade of "B," you must earn 35-40 points

- For a grade of "C," you must earn at least 25 points.

Lower grades are not acceptable. If you need assistance, please ask!

Activities that take only a short time to complete earn fewer points than activities that take more time and may involve doing some work outside of school.

- Activities #1, #2, #3, #4, and #5 are each worth 5 points

- Activities #6, #7, #8, #9, and #10 are each worth 10 points.

All students have an equal chance to earn a good grade for this unit.

All work must be completed by and handed in by _____.
                                                    DATE

It is expected that all products will be done carefully, and will be easy to read and/or understand. If you need help in judging whether your product meets these expectations, please ask your classmates.

# SUMMARY

In this chapter, you have learned how to create thematic, interdisciplinary units of instruction for all students that incorporate appropriate challenges for gifted kids. You have learned how to manage situations in which students are working on different tasks simultaneously. The first time you use the methods described here, the process may seem tedious and time-consuming. It helps to remember that creating more challenging tasks for gifted kids is not actually "wasted" time, since all students will eventually experience some of those activities. Also, as you use these methods again and again, it will take you less time to complete each unit.

Many teachers who already use whole language or thematic units find that planning purposefully to accommodate the needs of gifted kids leads to more sophisticated outcomes than less structured planning does. Eventually, many teachers choose this as their preferred method of planning thematic units, regardless of their overall general teaching style.

## MORE RESOURCES FOR TEACHERS

- Bloom, Benjamin, *et al. Taxonomy of Educational Objectives: Handbook of the Cognitive Domain.* New York: Longman, 1984.

   A detailed description of Bloom's Taxonomy.

- Engine-Uity, Ltd. Telephone (602) 997-7144.

- CAPs (Contract Activity Packages). Available from Learning Styles Network. Telephone (718) 990-6335.

- Martens, LaVida and Stan. *Dr. Marvel's Magnificent Mind Machine.* Minneapolis: Free Spirit Publishing Inc., 1992.

   "Bloom's Taxonomy for Kids" in eight full-color posters that connect in a series.

- Thinking Caps Inc. Telephone 1-800-529-5581.

   Sources of self-contained units for independent study using Bloom's Taxonomy. Call and request catalogs and/or brochures.

# READING INSTRUCTION FOR GIFTED STUDENTS

What kind of reading program are you using? How well is it meeting the needs of your gifted students? If you have students who are reading at advanced levels, is it okay to simply place them in a higher level book or class for reading? Do gifted students need a separate reading program? This chapter answers these and other questions. It also describes several activities that gifted students really enjoy as part of their total reading program.

## SCENARIO: LESHON

Leshon had failed fifth grade once, and he was now the tallest and biggest boy in his class. His former teachers described him as "lazy" because he never completed his homework in any subject. Some referred to his "poor attitude." Leshon refused to read the stories from the basal reader, never even opened his workbook, and had been overheard proclaiming, "I hate reading—it's dumb!" Over the years, he had spent many hours in the principal's office.

Leshon's new teacher noticed that he always had a magazine about cars or trucks hidden in his desk. Furthermore, it was a magazine written for adults! Leshon delighted in challenging his classmates to a contest of wits over the engine capacity and speed potential of the newest cars, and he seemed to have that information at his fingertips. It was obvious to his teacher that he was actually reading and understanding the material in his magazines. Yet he was still failing all of his classes, including reading.

One weekend, Leshon's teacher attended a seminar on the topic of teaching gifted students. While listening to the instructor describe some of the characteristic behaviors of gifted kids, she realized that she had observed many of those behaviors in Leshon.* Upon returning to school, the teacher arranged to meet with other teachers and the school principal. She asked them to tell her which students came to mind as she read aloud the list of characteristic behaviors. Leshon's name was mentioned over and over again. Could it be that his school problems were caused by boredom and frustration rather than "laziness" or a "poor attitude"?

---

*For a list of characteristic behaviors of gifted and talented students, see Appendix A, pages 139-140.

The teacher decided to test her theory by offering Leshon pretesting and compacting opportunities in several subjects. At first, Leshon seemed unable to believe that a teacher would allow him to demonstrate mastery by doing *less* work than he had previously been asked to do. And when he learned that he could spend class reading time with his magazines, as well as novels and books about car racing and race drivers, his eyes nearly popped out of his head.

The results were just short of miraculous. Within days, Leshon was back on the right learning track, completing his compacted work quickly and demonstrating a more positive attitude about school than anyone on staff had ever observed. His mother even commented to the teacher about the remarkable changes she was seeing in her son. After about two weeks, the principal dropped by the class to see if Leshon had been absent with some terrible illness. Since Leshon was no longer being sent to the office to be disciplined, the principal assumed the worst! Leshon's story provides ample evidence that modifying the curriculum can be a much more effective catalyst for change than behavior modification programs and punitive discipline methods.

# READING FOR GIFTED STUDENTS

Traditional basal reading programs have failed to meet the learning needs of many students, including the gifted. Most high ability students have already mastered the vocabulary and skills they will be expected to "learn" this year. They need opportunities to demonstrate their competencies, and to replace unnecessary work with meaningful reading experiences. If you are using a traditional approach that relies on a basal text and workbook, you should provide regular pretesting opportunities for all students. This allows you to see which vocabulary words and specific reading skills they have already mastered. Students who demonstrate mastery should be engaged in alternate reading activities at the same time as others in the class are doing the "regular work" from the basal reader and workbook. Ideas for alternate activities are presented throughout this chapter.

Perhaps you are using a "whole language" reading program. Whole language may be defined as the integration of all curricular areas that contribute to students' reading, writing, and speaking abilities. Subjects such as phonics, grammar, spelling, writing, listening, and recreational reading have been treated separately in most reading programs for many years. In a whole language program, they are combined through the study of a novel or a theme. Learning activities are designed so that all students are actively involved, frequently working with other students to learn together. Thematic units include activities from many subject areas.

If you are using a program labeled "whole language," you may need to make certain that it actually delivers a whole language philosophy. Some so-called "whole language" programs are really traditional skill-based programs in disguise. The reading program that is most appropriate for all students, and essential for gifted students, is one that allows them to read, discuss, analyze, and write about real literature, while being excused from practicing skills they have already mastered.

In some districts, the whole language philosophy has been misunderstood. Teachers have been informed that "whole language" means "whole class" instruction, and that no student should be allowed to use reading materials assigned to a higher grade level. Whole language programs were *never* intended to restrict students to materials that are too easy for them. Although there may be a good reason to prevent students from using basal texts assigned to different grade levels, their access to literature at all levels of reading should never be restricted. Some staffs have decided to earmark a limited number of novels for each grade level, and they have asked teachers to refrain from using books not assigned to their grade. When the number of "restricted" novels is limited to six or so, this practice is perfectly reasonable, since there is clearly an abundance of materials remaining from which teachers may choose.

Whenever possible, use your own best judgment about the appropriateness of instructional materials for students who are learning at a rate far above grade level. If your whole language program contains any components which don't seem valuable, you may decide to use the same compacting and individualizing opportunities described in this chapter and elsewhere in this book.

One of the most significant purposes of teaching reading is to generate a love of literature in children. Any classroom practices that accomplish that goal should be preferable to those that cause students to avoid reading and writing except when they are required. Talking to parents about their kids' attitudes toward reading at home, and observing the extent to which your students choose to read when they have opportunities to make choices, will give you valuable evidence about their reading attitudes. Incorporating highly motivating strategies, such as those presented in this chapter, will help you to keep your students enthusiastic about reading.

# STRATEGY FOR TRADITIONAL READING PROGRAMS: THE READING CONTRACT

When skills and vocabulary are taught separately, reading for gifted students may be managed by means of learning contracts, such as the type described in Chapter 3 for math instruction. Pretests are made available at the beginning of each section of the basal reader. Students who meet certain criteria work with the class for direct instruction *only* when the class is learning concepts the gifted students have not already mastered. During other times, they are free to select activities from a menu of alternatives. A sample reading contract is shown on page 86. Note that the top part of the contract may be completed using page numbers or concepts on workbook pages; both are shown on the sample to demonstrate options.

# STRATEGY FOR WHOLE LANGUAGE READING PROGRAMS: THE ACTIVITIES MENU

If you wish to provide alternate activities that extend the whole language unit for more capable students, consider an Activities Menu such as the one on page 88. Students who "buy back" time in reading may choose from a list of options. In addition, the menu allows "free" days on which students may create their own activities or continue with listed activities. The Activities Menu may be adapted for use with any subject by preparing appropriate activities. The Tic-Tac-Toe menu described in Chapter 5, pages 63-64, may also be used in this situation.

# STRATEGY FOR BASAL READING PROGRAMS: USING TRADE BOOKS

A less formal way to manage the alternate reading activities of gifted students is to encourage students to read literature of their choice, then discuss what they have read with one another and with you. They may all read the same novel, different books of the same genre or type, or books by the same author. Or you may decide to let each student read a completely different book. Following are strategies for managing these various options.

### All Reading the Same Novel

You might begin by asking several students to agree on a novel they would like to read together. Relate the vocabulary, writing activities, and other skill work to that novel. In some cases, you may be able to use selected pages from workbooks instead of having to create new activities. Meet with this group in much the same way you would with a typical reading group. The main difference is that your discussions and activities will be related to the novel instead of a selection from a basal reader.

Provide appropriately challenging activities. Following is a list of suggestions; feel free to add more of your own.

- Emphasize critical thinking activities.
- Connect related writing activities.
- Hypothesize on the validity of the content and events.
- Locate inferences, cause and effect, etc.
- Find foreshadowing, personification, other literary elements.
- Analyze the theme and its relationship to other books.
- Analyze the bias of characters and/or the author.
- Create a storytelling activity to share the story.
- Rewrite certain events or create a new ending.
- Write a similar story.
- Write the same story, set in a different time period.
- Read biographies about real people in similar situations to that described in the novel.

## CONTRACT FOR READING SKILLS AND VOCABULARY

STUDENT'S NAME: _____

_____ 58 (plurals)                              _____ 63 (suffixes)

_____ 59 (subject/verb agreement)               _____ 64 (suffixes)

_____ 60 (prefixes)                             _____ 65 (possessives)

_____ 61 (prefixes)                             _____ 66 (possessives)

_____ 62 (compound words)                       _____ 67 (parts of speech)

VOCABULARY WORDS FOR UNIT: Listed below are the words you need to study. Mastery of others was demonstrated on the pretest.

_____   _____   _____

_____   _____   _____

_____   _____   _____

### ALTERNATE ACTIVITIES

Record the way you spend your time while the rest of the class is working on concepts you have mastered. The only expectation is that you spend your time reading and/or writing.

| DATE | ACTIVITY |
|------|----------|
|      |          |
|      |          |
|      |          |
|      |          |

Teacher's Signature: _____ Student's Signature: _____

# HOW TO USE THE CONTRACT FOR READING SKILLS AND VOCABULARY

1. Offer a pretest on vocabulary and skills for the upcoming reading unit.

   Students who achieve a score of 80 percent or higher are eligible for a contract.

2. In the top third of the contract, list the relevant text page numbers or concepts.

   Check those that indicate concepts for which students must join the class for instruction. Tell students that they are not allowed to work on any checked item until it is taught to the class as a whole, at which time they must join the other students for a teacher-directed lesson.

3. In the middle third, list the vocabulary words the student has not yet mastered, as evidenced by pretest outcomes.

   Designate activities for the students to complete in order to learn the words.

4. On days when contract students don't have to be with the rest of the class for reading, they are to choose any activity that requires them to read and/or write.

   Tell them to keep a record of their activities in the chart on the bottom of the page. They are not required to complete a separate activity each time they work away from the class, but may return to work in progress.

5. Remind contract students that they must do their work without bothering anyone or calling attention to themselves.

   Make it clear that if they can't follow these guidelines, they will rejoin the class for the rest of the unit. For a more detailed list of working conditions for alternate activities, see Chapter 3, page 32.

- Research the life of a famous person and write an original biography.

- Compare and contrast books by the same author.

- Compare and contrast books of the same genre.

- Create a dramatic reading or short play about the story.

- Invent your own activity; discuss it with the teacher before you start working.

Don't be surprised if the group studying the novel expresses a great deal more excitement than the group working in the basal reader. If this happens in your classroom, you may decide to remove all students from the basal for a period of time and let the whole class study a novel. Students who finish reading it ahead of the others may use the remaining time to read other books by the same author or of the same genre. Their experience with the related literature will enhance the discussions of the assigned book.

### *All Reading Different Novels by the Same Author*

If you choose this option, you may want to use a cooperative learning format. Put the gifted students together in one group and allow them to choose a more complex novel. Removing them from the other groups will force the rest of the students to work more actively. Also, when gifted students are allowed to work in their own cooperative group, they are more likely to participate in cooperative activities than when they are in a group that slows down their reading pace and limits their preferred complexity of thought and discussion. For more about gifted kids and cooperative learning, see Chapter 9.

Meet with each group separately to discuss their particular novel. Discussions about the author's style may take place with the entire class. Again, the excitement and enthusiasm of the students may motivate you to replace some basal reader activities with even more literature experiences. Some teachers use this method as a transition to a whole language program, setting aside one day of the week for literature study while staying with the basal for the other four days. Soon one day becomes two, two become three, and eventually these teachers are using a whole language approach entirely and permanently. In some schools, teachers are allowed to use the money that has been budgeted for basals

# ACTIVITIES MENU

Name _____

## DIRECTIONS:

During the next _____ days, create your own menu of activities from the list below to do in place of the regular assignments.

| Date(s) | Activity | Date(s) | Activity |
|---|---|---|---|
| _____ | Puppet show of story or book | _____ | Create a dialogue between 2 characters |
| _____ | Interview another person who read book | _____ | Read other books by same author; compare/contrast |
| _____ | Write letter to author | _____ | Read another book of the same type; compare/contrast |
| _____ | Write another chapter | | |
| _____ | Write a different ending | _____ | Write a story or book of the same type which contains similar elements |
| _____ | Find synonyms of your 6 favorite words | | |

Include 3 "free" days—you create the activity or add on days to activities above.

| Date | Activity |
|---|---|
|  |  |

and workbooks to buy literature books and other whole language support materials.

### All Reading Different Novels of the Same Genre

As an extension of a unit in a basal reader, you might set aside time for all students to read library books or trade books of the same type or genre. For example, if your class has just finished a unit on folk tales, your students might choose to read folk tales from different countries. You could select four to six titles, and your students would work in cooperative groups as described above. Or you might allow students to choose their own folk tale titles. Class discussions would center around the characteristics of the genre, and students would contribute to the discussion based on what they had read individually.

### Individualized Reading

To meet the needs of gifted students—and elevate *all* students' interest in reading—consider letting everyone read a different book. You will want to have a variety of titles, topics, and reading levels available in the classroom. Several publishing companies distribute collections for this purpose, including Scholastic, McDougall Littell, and Rigby.*

---

## HOW TO USE THE ACTIVITIES MENU

1. Prepare a menu of activities from which students may choose several they would like to do.

2. Tell students that they may choose an activity to work on during the times you designate. They may continue working on their activity until it is completed.

3. Have students record the dates they *begin* and *end* an activity on the Date(s) line. (Example: "October 5-October 7.")

4. If students have original ideas for projects or activities, they should discuss them with you before starting to work on them. After you give your permission for a specific project or activity, the student should record it in the blank space at the bottom of the menu.

---

Initially, students should be free to browse through any books that interest them. Advise them to use the "Rule of Three" to select any book they actually plan to read. Tell them, "Open the book to some page in the middle—preferably a page without pictures—and start reading. Whenever you come across a word you don't know, hold up one finger. When your count exceeds three words on one page, the book is probably too difficult for you to read independently. Go to another book and try again."

There are many ways for students to keep track of what they read. For example, they can tally the types of books they read on the Circle of Books shown on page 90. As students finish reading a book, they place a tally mark in the appropriate section of the wheel. The marks help them to see if they are reading from a variety of categories or limiting themselves to one or two. Naturally, you may use other categories than the ones shown.

Another method is to use a reading response journal, usually kept in a separate spiral notebook. To use a reading response journal, students spend a few minutes after each reading period jotting down their thoughts about the book, including their reactions to events and characters, predictions about upcoming events, character studies, rewritten chapters or endings, etc. In a section at the back, they record up to ten words per book that they find especially interesting or curious. You may suggest activities that will help the students learn these words, or the students may discuss them when they meet with other students who are doing individualized reading.

I recommend that you keep an ongoing record sheet for each individualized reading student. You'll find a form you can copy and use on page 92. Schedule weekly conferences, and tell students that they must meet with you on their scheduled day whether or not they have completed their books. If they need a conference on a different day, they may sign up at a specified place on the chalkboard. Before each conference ends, schedule the *next* conference, and note the date on the student's record sheet. This helps you to keep track of when students are expected to return, and also makes it harder for students to "forget" to come to conferences for long periods of time.

---

*Call toll-free to request catalogs from Scholastic (1-800-822-5110), McDougall Littell (1-800-323-5435), and Rigby (1-800-822-8661).

# THE CIRCLE OF BOOKS

Each time you finish a book, put a tally mark in the appropriate section. Check to see if you are reading from a variety of categories, or limiting yourself to just one or two.

Fiction | Biography | Mystery | Adventure | Humor | Science Fiction | Fantasy | Animals

Provide a way for students to share their books with one another. Avoid formal written book reports, since these generally have a negative effect on students' attitudes about reading. There are many alternatives to book reports that are far more creative and fun. For example, you might hold a regularly scheduled Book Sharing Time, during which students report verbally and briefly (two to three minutes) about a book they are currently reading or have recently completed.

Each student begins by writing the author's name or the book's call number on the board. Next, the student says the title, but doesn't write it.* Listeners don't write anything until after the speaker has finished sharing. At the end, the speaker announces the author's name or the book's call number again, and repeats the title. By now, listeners have decided if this is a book they might want to read. If it is, they record the information in their reading response journal, on a separate sheet of paper, or on a form designed for this purpose, such as the one on page 94. The next time they go to the library to select books, they carry their lists with them. Since they already know what books they want, they can usually find them without anybody's help.

Another excellent way for students to share their reading is through a Recommended Books Chart. A model chart is shown on page 96. Use it to create a larger chart—at least 24" x 36"—to post on a wall or bulletin board. Hang a pencil on a string nearby, and watch the chart fill up with student recommendations. Encourage the students to use "soft voices" at the chart, which is sure to become a center for discussion about books and authors.

A third way for students to share their reading is with Book Logos. Assign each student a certain color paper and keep supplies of each color in labeled folders. Make a chart like the one on page 97, laminate it to prevent fading, and post it in the classroom. When a student finishes a book, he or she takes a piece of the colored paper, cuts it out in a shape that represents an event or character from the book, prints the title and author's name in black marker on the "logo," and displays it in some way.

One year, in one fifth-grade class, 27 students read 384 books! The logos were displayed in a line near the ceiling of the room, which eventually spilled out into the hall and wound its way around the entire floor. Imagine the lively conversations about books that were stimulated by the presence of these colorful logos. Furthermore, if students wanted to recommend certain books they had read to other students, they could easily locate the appropriate logo by its color. This method of keeping track of the books your students read is certainly preferable to the traditional chart, which demonstrates (sometimes painfully) who the sluggish readers are for all the world to see. An observer would have to work to add up the number of books read by a particular student. And since the purpose of the logos is to provide a forum for discussing books, nobody really cares about the numbers anyway.

# VOCABULARY BUILDING ACTIVITIES

Gifted kids usually love vocabulary work, once they are introduced to the magic of words. All gifted students should have their own thesauruses for regular use in their writing. To get your whole class hooked on words, bring in a copy of a "how-to-name-your-baby" book. Students will become fascinated with the history of their own names. Once they've been enticed by that, they are likely to be excited about studying the history of other words as well.

Working with the children's librarian or reader's service librarian at a public library, you can collect a variety of materials that help kids experience the delights of playing with words, understanding how words change through time, and learning how new words are added to our language. Look for books that help you teach one or more of the topics listed on page 98. Introduce one category at a time, giving several examples. Then challenge students to come up with at least ten more examples in the same category. Since gifted kids are highly competitive, they will work very quietly on these so nobody else steals their ideas!

Reproducible forms for vocabulary building activities are found on pages 98, 99, 100, 102, and 104.

---

*Not having the speaker write the title on the board saves time. If listeners have either the correct spelling of the author's last name, or the correct call number, they can easily find the book, even if they use invented spelling to record the title.

# TEACHER'S CONFERENCE RECORD SHEET

Student's Name: _____

| Date | Book | Conference Discussion | Assigned Tasks Teacher Notes |
|------|------|----------------------|------------------------------|
|      |      |                      |                              |
|      |      |                      |                              |
|      |      |                      |                              |
|      |      |                      |                              |
|      |      |                      |                              |
|      |      |                      |                              |
|      |      |                      |                              |
|      |      |                      |                              |

# HOW TO USE THE TEACHER'S CONFERENCE RECORD SHEET

1. Record the date of each conference in the far left column.

2. Record the name of the student's book in the "Book" column.

3. Make notes of the conference discussion in the third column. Questions and suggestions for sparking and guiding the discussion include:

   - What is this story about?
   - What techniques does the author use to "hook" you?
   - What's the best part? Why? The worst/most boring part? Why?
   - Find a good descriptive passage and read it to me.
   - How did you feel about the characters?
   - How does the author get you to feel close to the characters?
   - Which character was the most well developed? The least?
   - Say and define some of the interesting vocabulary words you found.
   - Were there any parts that didn't seem to belong in the book?
   - What did you admire about the author's style that you might use in your own writing?
   - Was there anything confusing about the author's style? Explain.
   - How would you change the book? The ending?
   - What will you highlight on the Recommended Books Chart? (See page 96.)

4. In the far right column, note any tasks you ask the student to complete. These may be related to vocabulary development, story mapping, character study, or anything else you would normally use to teach a story.

5. Before the conference ends, note the date of the *next* conference on the new line.

# BOOKS I WANT TO READ

This List Belongs To _____

| CALL NUMBER OR AUTHOR'S NAME | TITLE OF BOOK | WHAT BOOK IS ABOUT |
|---|---|---|
| | | |
| | | |
| | | |
| | | |
| | | |
| | | |
| | | |
| | | |
| | | |
| | | |

# HOW TO USE THE BOOKS I WANT TO READ CHART

1. Give all students a copy of the chart. Instruct them to keep it in their desk or reading folder at all times. It *never* goes home!

2. Tell students to have this chart out on their desks during each Book Sharing Time. They should use the same chart until it is full. You'll give them a new one to staple to their old one(s).

3. Instruct students to listen as the speaker shares information about a book. They should not write anything until after the speaker has finished.

4. Students who decide that they want to read the book should write the author's name or the book's call number on their chart, along with the title (invented spelling is okay). The column on the right is optional for the student to record information about the book.

5. When your class goes to the library to select books, make sure they carry their charts with them.

6. Tell students to cross books off their list as they finish reading them to avoid searching for a book they have already read.

| Your Name | Name of Book | Author; Call Number | Why I'm Recommending It | People I Think Would Like This Book |
|---|---|---|---|---|
| | | | | |
| | | | | |
| | | | | |
| | | | | |
| | | | | |
| | | | | |
| | | | | |
| | | | | |
| | | | | |
| | | | | |

**RECOMMENDED BOOKS CHART**

# HOW TO USE THE RECOMMENDED BOOKS CHART

1. Using the chart above as a model, create a large (at least 24" x 36") chart to display in the classroom. Provide a pencil on a string so students always have something to write with.

2. Show students how to enter information on the chart.

3. Decide what criteria students must meet to enter a book on the chart. For example: Did they read the book in another class or year? Are they reading it now, but haven't finished it yet? Did they recently finish reading it?

4. Encourage students to use "soft voices" at the chart.

## BOOK LOGOS CHART

The actual chart will show samples of the color paper assigned to each student, not the names of the colors.

| Student's Name | Color Assigned | Student's Name | Color Assigned |
|---|---|---|---|
| Jason | Navy blue | Eric | Ivory |
| Tom | Red | Leandra | Gold |
| Kyoko | Gray | Joey | Violet |
| Susie | Yellow | Roberto | Neon yellow |
| Leshon | Orange | Elizabeth | Purple |
| Barbra | Pastel pink | Jim | Neon green |
| José | Brown | Julie | Neon pink |
| James | Black | Dimitri | Light blue |
| Alicia | Turquoise | Elena | Green |

## HOW TO USE BOOK LOGOS

1. Locate as many colors of paper as you have students in your room. Then add three or four more so you're ready for new students who move in later.

2. Cut the sheets of colored paper into 8 1/2" x 11" pieces, if they are not already that size. Then cut them in half again. Pieces should be 4 1/4" x 5 1/2".

3. Prepare two sample swatches of each color and place *one* of each into a "hat." All swatches should be the same size.

4. Have students select their color by drawing sample pieces from the "hat." Tell them to write their name on their color and give it back to you.

5. Glue the appropriate swatch beside each student's name on the Book Logos Chart. Laminate the chart before displaying it, or the sun's fading powers will make the colors unrecognizable in a few days. Display the chart in the classroom, perhaps near the Recommended Books Chart (see page 96).

6. Prepare a folder for each student, filled with a supply of his or her color paper. Label each folder with the student's name and the second color swatch.

7. Direct the students to make a logo for each book they finish reading.

   *Instructions:* "Cut out a shape from a piece of your paper that represents the essence of your book. This is your 'logo' for that book. Using dark colored marker, print only the name of the book and the author on your logo."

8. Display the logos around the room. When you run out of space, display them in the hallways.

9. Students may show their logos when they talk about their books to the class.

10. You might tell prolific readers to make a logo for every third or fourth book they read. If they have to make too many logos, they might get turned off to reading.

# VOCABULARY BUILDERS

1. ACRONYMS: Words made of the first letters of things people want to remember.

   *Examples:* "HOMES" for the names of the Great Lakes (Huron, Ontario, Michigan, Erie, Superior); "NEWS" for the directions on a compass (North, East, West, South).

2. COINED WORDS: Words people create to fill a need that no existing word describes precisely.

   *Examples:* Many slang words fit this category. Which words are popular with you and your friends? Challenge yourself to coin new words. What about a single word to replace both "he" and "she"?

3. DAFFYNITIONS: Crazy definitions for phrases.

   *Examples:* "Grapes grow on...divine." "Police uniform = lawsuit."

4. ETYMOLOGIES: The histories of words: their origins and changes through time.

   *Example:* "Bonfire" came from the fire that was set to burn the bodies of people who died in the Bubonic Plague in the 15th century. Its original meaning was "bone fire."

   *NOTE:* Your teacher will give you a separate form for this activity.

5. EUPHEMISMS: Softer ways of saying things that sound too harsh or impolite.

   *Example:* "He passed away at an early age" instead of "He died young."

6. FIGURES OF SPEECH: Expressions that mean something different than what they say literally.

   *Example:* "There are many skeletons in our family closet."

7. PALINDROMES: Words that are spelled the same forward and backward

   *Examples:* "Deed," "Otto," "madam."

8. PORTMANTEAUS: Words made by blending parts of other words.

   *Example:* "Brunch" from "breakfast" and "lunch."

9. PREFIXES AND SUFFIXES FROM LATIN OR GREEK ROOTS

   *Examples:* "Pre-" (before), "-ist" (one who)

10. PUNS: Plays on words

    *Example:* "Those *pancakes* are selling like *hotcakes*."

11. SLIDE WORDS: Words made from abbreviations.

    *Example:* "Jeep" from "g-p," which meant "general purpose vehicle" during World War II.

12. SUPER SENTENCES: Sentences with complex words that need to be translated into simpler language.

    *NOTE:* Your teacher will give you a separate form for this activity. You'll also need an unabridged dictionary.

13. TOM SWIFTIES: Statements that combine a verb and a related modifier.

    *Examples:* "I just *cut* my finger," said Tom *sharply*. "I'm so terribly *thirsty*," complained Tom *dryly*.

14. TRANSMOGRIFIED WORDS: Very fancy words for simple thoughts.

    *Examples:* "Scintillate, scintillate, asteroid minific" for "Twinkle, twinkle, little star." Try transmogrifying mottoes, proverbs, nursery rhymes, and the names of favorite TV shows and movies. Or challenge yourself with a transmogrified story. First, find a story to "translate." Next, write a one-page summary. Use a thesaurus to rewrite the story in fancy words. Have a competition with your friends; the winner is the student whose story takes the others the longest to figure out!

# ETYMOLOGIES ACTIVITIES

## The History of Words

**1.** Meanings of 10 first names—either gender.

**2.** People's last names that describe occupations.
**Examples:** Hooper, Smith, Taylor.

**3.** Places or things named after people.
**Examples:** Mansard roof, Sideburns, Sandwich Islands (named for the Earl of Sandwich).

**4.** Native American words or names.

**5.** Foreign words in common English usage.

**6.** Words or phrases from sports.
**Examples:** Strike out, take a new tack.

**7.** Any other words or phrases that interest you.

**8.** Words or phrases from a new category you create.

RECOMMENDED RESOURCES:

- *A Second Browser's Dictionary* by John Ciardi (New York: Harper and Row, 1983)

- *Thereby Hangs a Tale: Stories of Curious Word Origins* by Charles Funk (New York: Harper and Row, 1985)

- *Morris Dictionary of Word and Phrase Origins* by William Morris and Mary Morris (New York: Harper and Row, 1977)

- *I've Got Goose Pimples* by Marvin Vanoni (New York: William Morrow, 1989).

# ETYMOLOGIES CHART

CATEGORY: _____

| Word or Phrase | Original Language | Meaning in Original Language | Today's Meaning | Sentence |
|---|---|---|---|---|
| | | | | |
| | | | | |
| | | | | |

# HOW TO USE THE ETYMOLOGIES CHART

1. Invite students to select a category from those listed on the "Etymologies Activities" handout (page 99).

2. Instruct them to find 10 or more examples to fit their category. Try to have several college or unabridged dictionaries in your classroom for the students to use.

3. Explain how to complete the chart. Students should write the *word or phrase* they are investigating in the far left column; the *original language* of the word or phrase in the next column; the *meaning in the original language* of the word or phrase in the next column; and *today's meaning* in the next column. In the far right column, they should write an original *sentence* using the word or phrase. Rebus sentences may sometimes be used in place of word sentences.

4. Have students use a separate chart for each category they investigate.

# SUPER SENTENCE: LEVEL ONE

**Directions:** Work with a partner to pronounce and define each "mystery word" (words in capital letters), read the sentence as it appears, and translate it into simpler words.

We live near a GROTESQUE, HIDEOUS, DETERIORATED old house, filled with TORTUOUS, IMPENETRABLE hallways which give me EERIE, GHASTLY feelings of CLAUSTROPHOBIA and TREPIDATION, especially when I hear the FORMIDABLE CACOPHONY of BABBLING voices when no one is there.

| Word | Pronunciation | Meaning |
|------|---------------|---------|
|  |  |  |
|  |  |  |
|  |  |  |
|  |  |  |
|  |  |  |
|  |  |  |
|  |  |  |
|  |  |  |
|  |  |  |
|  |  |  |
|  |  |  |
|  |  |  |

Translation: _____

_____

# WRITING OPPORTUNITIES

Writing opportunities should be expanded for all students into all subject areas. When you "experiment" first with gifted students, it becomes obvious that they can enjoy writing, and even ask for it as an activity of choice! Once the spark is ignited by the gifted students, it's easier to create similar expanded writing opportunities for other students as well.

Many gifted students write stories, poems, and plays and keep them at home. It's always a good idea to have these kids keep an ongoing writing project in class to which they can return whenever they buy some free time. Many of the great writing ideas you've used over the years are greatly enjoyed by gifted kids. Remember, they usually enjoy taking an idea and then adapting or changing it in some way to make it "theirs."

It's important for kids who enjoy writing to have opportunities to submit their work for publication. Classroom and school newsletters are okay, but when you find something that's really exceptional, you should look for a "real" outlet for the work. Student writers should contact publishers themselves by writing a formal letter of inquiry—terrific experience for their budding writing careers. The names and addresses of several publications that welcome children's writing are listed below and on page 105.*

Child Life
PO Box 567
1100 Waterway Boulevard
Indianapolis, IN 46206
*All types; ages 7-9*

Children's Album
EGW Publishing Co.
1320 Galaxy Way
Concord, CA 94520
*Children's crafts and creative writing; all ages*

Creative Kids
Prufrock Press
PO Box 8813
Waco, TX 76714
*Stories, poems, art, and music; all ages*

Merlyn's Pen
98 Main Street, Box 1058
Greenwich, RI 02818
1-800-247-2027
*Plays, short stories, and poetry; grades 7-10*

*More publishers of children's writing are listed in *Market Guide for Young Writers*, 4th edition, by Kathy Henderson (Cincinnati, OH: Writer's Digest Books, 1993).

# HOW TO USE SUPER SENTENCES

*NOTE:* Students work in pairs.

1. Read the sentence aloud several times. Tell students to listen carefully and try to determine the parts of speech for the capitalized words. They should write the part of speech above each capitalized word to make sure they select the correct dictionary entry.

2. Instruct the students to work with their partners (and unabridged dictionaries) to complete the chart. Tell them to list the "mystery words" (those in capital letters) in the far left column, write the pronunciation of each word in the center column (using the pronunciation key from a dictionary), and write the meaning of the word in the far right column—*in their own words.*

3. To complete this activity, students must be able to pronounce and define each capitalized word, read the sentence as it appears, and "translate" it into simpler words.

4. When they are ready, or after at least 5 days of work, bring the pairs together in a circle.
   - The first student reads the sentence up to and including the first capitalized word.
   - The next student starts where the first student stops, and reads all words up to and including the next capitalized word.
   - Students keep taking turns until someone asks to read the entire sentence aloud.
   - When several students have read it aloud, the sentence should be "translated" and reread in simpler words.

# SUPER SENTENCE: LEVEL TWO

**Directions:** Work with a partner to pronounce and define each "mystery word" (words in capital letters), read the sentence as it appears, and translate it into simpler words.

The TRUCULENT, OPPIDAN LICKSPITTLE SEQUESTERED himself from the BROUHAHA caused by the PUSILLANIMOUS MOUNTEBANK, and MACHINATED a MACHIAVELLIAN PREVARICATION to METE to himself some of the mountebank's LUCRE.

| Word | Pronunciation | Meaning |
|------|---------------|---------|
|      |               |         |
|      |               |         |
|      |               |         |
|      |               |         |
|      |               |         |
|      |               |         |
|      |               |         |
|      |               |         |
|      |               |         |
|      |               |         |
|      |               |         |

Translation: _____

_____

# MORE RESOURCES FOR TEACHERS

- Brody, Linda, Susan Assouline, and Julian Stanley. "Five Years of Early Entrants: Predicting Successful Achievement in College." *Gifted Child Quarterly* 34:4 (1990).

     Documents that early entrance to kindergarten for profoundly gifted kids is a positive response to their need for acceleration.

- Colangelo, Nicholas, and Gary Davis. *Handbook of Gifted Education.* Needham Heights, MA: Allyn and Bacon, 1991.

- Feldhusen, John, Theron Proctor, and Kathryn Black. "Guidelines for Early Entrance into Kindergarten." West Lafayette, IN: Purdue University, 1988.

     Guidelines for schools to use in deciding which students should be allowed early admission to kindergarten.

Helpful resources especially for parents of gifted children:

- *Understanding Our Gifted.* PO Box 3489, Littleton, CO 80122.

     Bimonthly newsletter dedicated to helping gifted children reach their full potential.

- Alvino, James. *Parents' Guide to Raising a Gifted Child.* New York: Ballantine, 1985.

- Rimm, Sylvia. *How to Parent So Children Will Learn.* Watertown, WI: Apple Publishing Company, 1990. 1-800-475-1118.

- Walker, Sally. *The Survival Guide for Parents of Gifted Kids.* Minneapolis, MN: Free Spirit Publishing Inc., 1991.

- Webb, James, Elizabeth Meckstroth, and Stephanie Tolan. *Guiding the Gifted Child.* Columbus, OH: Ohio Psychology Publishing Co., 1982.

# CONCLUSION

**T**his book comes with my personal guarantee that the strategies it contains really work! The teachers I have trained over many years report dramatic success.

- Students with exceptional ability who have previously been nonproductive rise to the challenge of the pretests, the Most Difficult First technique, the Topic Browsing Planner, the resident expert opportunity, and other strategies. They do a significant turnaround in terms of attitude and effort.

- Gifted students who have been successful in school enjoy bringing their "real life" interests to class and working as junior researchers on satisfying projects.

- Teachers are pleased and excited to note their gifted students' enthusiastic acceptance of the new opportunities, and to see so many of their other students also benefiting from the strategies.

Sometimes we may think that gifted students must first learn the lesson that "in the real world, people don't get to do what they want all the time." We may perceive that our job is to prepare these kids to "fit in" to the reality of daily life as an adult. We tell ourselves that it may be "good for them" to experience some boredom and frustration in school. Unfortunately, this approach may create more problems than it solves.

Many people who started life as gifted students go through adulthood behaving more average than gifted. One reason may be that they have lost faith in the excitement of learning and have come to believe the "real life" lessons well-meaning adults tried to teach them in their youth. What are we accomplishing by teaching these students how to deal with boredom? What if, instead, we gave them the chance to enjoy learning, and to develop the important study skills that accompany hard work?

Dr. Sylvia Rimm teaches that "the surest path to high self-esteem is to be successful at something one perceived would be *difficult*." Most teachers believe that helping students develop positive self-esteem is an important part of our job. When we teach gifted students, the best way to guarantee their secure self-esteem (as well as their appropriate humbleness) is to provide them with the challenge that most other students receive each day in school: the challenge to learn something new, and to discover firsthand that struggling to learn can be exciting.

With this in mind, the best advice I can give you is to try some of the strategies in this book with at least *one* student who has clearly been nonproductive compared to how you perceive his or her potential ability. Perhaps nothing you have tried so far has motivated this student to do quality work. Try at least *one* of these techniques with him or her, and see what happens next. If your experience is the same as that of many other teachers, you will be delighted to discover that providing appropriately differentiated curricula for gifted students is neither mysterious nor difficult. And the joy shared by you, the student, and his or her parents as the student's love of learning is rekindled will be reward enough for your efforts.

The whole purpose of this book, and of all the strategies contained in it, is to help you create opportunities for gifted students to use school time for work that represents true learning for them. When we set up situations where students first have to do *our* work before they can do *their* work, we invite the passive-aggressive behaviors that have the potential to drive us crazy! These behaviors include working so slowly that it seems the student will *never* finish, "forgetting" assignments, careless work habits, poor attitude, etc. Consciously or not, frustrated gifted students use these negative behaviors to communicate, "I don't need this, and I don't want this. But you can make me do it because you have the power. So I'm going to behave in ways that will make it a little more bearable for me—and a little less bearable for you."

On the other hand, when we use the methods described in this book, we demonstrate an understanding of our gifted students' unique learning needs, and a respect for their genuine learning differences. Instead of wasting their time (and ours), our students get down to the business of learning. Everybody wins.

While you were reading through this book, you may have discovered educational practices that were new to you. New practices will continue to emerge, and you may wonder whether your gifted students will benefit from being engaged with them. When in doubt, ask yourself, "Will applying this strategy uniformly to everyone in my class be educationally appropriate for my gifted students?" If the answer is no, then ask yourself, "How can I take the essence of what I'm expected to do and adjust it for gifted students so the instructional experiences represent true learning for them? How can I remember to give these kids more control over the daily tasks they do in my class?"

Here's how, in a series of 12 simple guidelines for teaching gifted kids in the regular classroom.

1. First, find out what they already know.

2. Give them "credit" for the concepts they have mastered.

3. Don't have them repeat grade level work just because it's there.

4. Provide alternate challenging activities for them to do instead of drill-and-practice or grade level work. Provide opportunities for them to work with complex and abstract ideas.

5. Discover what their interests are, and build their projects around their interests.

6. Allow them some flexibility in the way they use the time they "buy back."

7. Allow them to learn at a faster pace than their age peers.

8. Use discovery learning techniques often; avoid lecture and other teacher dominated methods.

9. *Trust them* to learn in nontraditional ways.

10. Help them to find kids just like themselves. Never judge their social skills solely on the way they interact with their age peers.

11. Thrill them with *choices, choices,* and *more choices.*

12. Give them lots of experience with setting their own goals and evaluating their own work.

ENJOY THE RESULTS!

Good luck! I sincerely hope that these strategies work for you, and I would love it if you would write to me about your experiences. Share other ideas you have used that work as well or better. I would even like to hear about strategies I suggested that *don't* work for you. Please give me the pertinent details, and I'll try to respond. You may write to me at the following address: Susan Winebrenner, c/o Free Spirit Publishing Inc., 400 First Avenue North, Suite 616, Minneapolis, MN 55401.

Thank you for choosing this book, and for trusting yourself enough to risk making school exciting for your gifted students.

# CHARACTERISTIC BEHAVIORS OF GIFTED AND TALENTED STUDENTS

Gifted students may exhibit many, but not all, of these characteristics. When you observe students consistently exhibiting these behaviors, the possibility that they are gifted is very strong. Trust your own observations more than the "evidence" of mediocre standardized test scores or poor grades.

## GENERAL

- Advanced vocabulary for chronological age

- Outstanding memory; possesses lots of information

- Curious; asks endless questions ("why?" "and then what?")

- Has many interests, hobbies, and collections

- May have a "passionate interest" that has lasted for many years (example: dinosaurs)

- Intense; gets totally absorbed in activities and thoughts

- Strongly motivated to do things that interest her; may be unwilling to work on other activities

- May be reluctant to move from one subject area to another

- Operates on higher levels of thinking than his age peers; is comfortable with abstract thinking

- Perceives subtle cause-and-effect relationships

- Prefers complex and challenging tasks to "basic" work

- May be able to "track" two or more things simultaneously (example: her daydreams and your words)

- Catches on quickly, then resists doing work, or works in a sloppy, careless manner

- Comes up with "better ways" for doing things; suggests them to peers, teachers, and other adults

- Sensitive to beauty and other people's feelings and emotions

- Advanced sense of justice and fairness

- Aware of global issues many age peers are uninterested in

- Sophisticated sense of humor; may be "class clown"

- Transfers concepts and learning to new situations

- Sees connections between apparently unconnected ideas and activities

- May prefer the company of older children or adults

- May prefer to work alone; resists cooperative learning

- Bossy in group situations

- Needs to constantly share all he knows; impatient when not called on to recite or respond

- May be "street smart" while not doing well on school tasks

## CREATIVE THINKING

- Displays original ideas

- Sees endless possibilities for various situations or uses for objects

- Says what she thinks without regard for consequences

- Brilliant thinker, but absentminded about details or where his work might be found

- Outstanding sense of humor; loves to play with words and ideas

- Passionately interested in some topic or field of endeavor

- May be talented in the fine arts

- Fluent in idea generation and development

- Able to elaborate on ideas

- Experiments with ideas and hunches

- Great imagination; frequent daydreamer

- Values nonconformity in appearance, thought, etc.

- Standardized test scores may be significantly better than class performance

## PERFECTIONISM

- Believes he is valued for what he can do rather than who he is.

- Has been praised consistently for her "greatness and exceptional ability."

- Fears he will lose the regard of others if he loses that exceptionality.

- May cry easily in frustration that her work at school can never be perfect.

- Works very slowly in hopes that his product will be perfect.

- Discovers a mistake in her work; erases until there is a hole in the paper or crumples up paper and throws it away.

- Asks for lots of help and reassurance from the teacher. ("Is this all right? Is this what you want? Please repeat the directions.")

- Cannot take any criticism or suggestions for improvement without being defensive.

- Expects other people to be perfect, too.

- Resists challenging work for fear his struggle will be seen by others. ("If my teacher and peers see me struggle, they will conclude I'm not so smart.")

- Procrastinates to the point that work never even gets started.

# ACTIVITIES FOR GIFTED STUDENTS

## CATEGORIES CHALLENGE

Sample chart A on page 142 is for use with the entire class; sample chart B on page 142 is for use with gifted students.

***Directions for the Entire Class:***

Create a chart for students to use. Write letters in the left column, and categories across the top. Choose categories that represent topics and materials with which the students are already familiar. The letters will be the first letters of their responses. (Examples: For "Birds," responses might include Mallard, Starling, Rooster, Tern, and Parrot.)

Divide the class into teams of four to five students. Tell them to work together to complete as many boxes on the chart as designated time allows (usually 15-20 minutes).

*Scoring:* The team that has the most correct responses at the end of the designated time is the winner. Don't just tell the class which responses are correct. Instead, read them aloud and have the students decide. Since all teams must rely on one another's fairness in this step, students are usually generous in their judgments.

***Directions for Gifted Students:***

Create a chart for students to use. Write letters in the left column, and categories across the top. Choose categories that represent topics and materials with which the students are generally *not* familiar. The letters will be the first letters of their responses.

Divide the students into teams of four. Tell the students to each pick a category, then work alone to complete as many boxes in that column as designated time allows (usually 20-30 minutes). Students will probably need to use reference materials to complete their categories.

When everyone is finished, the students work in teams to complete the fifth category. This is often the category with which they are *least* familiar, which is why they didn't choose to work on it alone.

*Variation:* One category or letter is free choice.

*Scoring:* Use the scoring method described above for the entire class.

| CATEGORIES CHALLENGE A: FOR THE ENTIRE CLASS | | | | |
|---|---|---|---|---|
| | BIRDS | BOOK TITLES | MAMMALS | U.S. STATES | TEACHERS |
| M | | | | | |
| S | | | | | |
| R | | | | | |
| T | | | | | |
| P | | | | | |

| CATEGORIES CHALLENGE B: FOR GIFTED STUDENTS IN THEIR OWN TEAMS | | | | |
|---|---|---|---|---|
| | U.S. PRESIDENTS | WORLD RIVERS | POETS' LAST NAMES | PRECIOUS STONES | INVENTORS |
| M | | | | | |
| P | | | | | |
| D | | | | | |
| E | | | | | |
| F | | | | | |

# CLASSROOM ACADEMIC BOWL

## *Preparing for Play:*

Divide students into teams of 4-6 students. Make sure that teams are heterogeneous, with one or two high-ability students, one student who has trouble learning, and the balance from those considered to be more average. Teams stay together for 4-6 weeks, until everyone has had the chance to be captain. The role of captain rotates each week.

Prepare two sets of questions: easier *entry questions*, and more difficult *bonus questions.*

- Entry questions are worth 5 points and may represent previously learned material the class is reviewing. Or you may choose to use easier trivia questions, such as those found in many popular games.

- Bonus questions are worth 10 points and may represent material the class is still trying to master. Or you may select more difficult trivia questions from popular games.

The quotations on pages 144-146 may be used for this game. Also, many students enjoy opportunities to create questions and answers for this game during time they "buy" from regular classroom activities.

The team that answers an entry question correctly earns the right to attempt the more difficult bonus questions and earn additional points.

You, the teacher, ask all of the questions and keep track of each team's score *privately*. In other words, don't display the scores for all to see until the game has ended. This gives you some flexibility in calling on teams to keep the outcome somewhat even.

## *Playing the Game:*

1. Set and describe the conditions for play. Explain the two levels of questions and their point values. Emphasize that *no points are lost for incorrect answers.* Tell students that the *only* way they can lose points is by making uncomplimentary remarks or gestures to other students, or by talking with teammates at times other than when they are supposed to confer to select a team response to a bonus question.

2. Begin by asking an entry question. Students raise their hands individually, and you call on someone. That person has five seconds to give an answer *without any help* from other students. If the student answers correctly, award five points to that team. If the student answers incorrectly, call on someone from another team. *No points are lost for incorrect answers.*

3. When a student answers an entry question correctly, give that team the opportunity to answer a bonus question. The team may confer for 15 seconds, and the answer may be stated *only by the team captain.* In this way, even shy students are eventually involved in the action—when they become team captain. If the captain answers correctly, award *ten points* to that team. If the captain answers incorrectly, call on students from other teams until someone gives the right answer. Award *five points* to that team. Again, *no points are lost for incorrect answers.*

4. At the end of the designated time, announce the points earned by each team. The team with the most points wins.

# QUOTATIONS FOR CLASSROOM ACADEMIC BOWL AND OTHER TRIVIA GAMES

Following are over 100 quotations suitable for trivia games. There are several possible ways to use them, depending on how you give them to your students (whole or in parts, with authors identified or not identified, etc.).

For example:

1. Read the first half of a quotation. Invite students to supply the ending.

2. Ask questions about the quotations. Example: "Whose quotation has to do with fear?"

3. Read a quotation aloud and ask who said it.

4. Have students find related quotations and add them to the list.

5. Ask student volunteers to discover information about the authors and under what circumstances the quotations came about.

*Joseph Addison*
"Reading is to the mind...what exercise is to the body."

*Louisa May Alcott*
"There is not much danger that real talent or goodness will be overlooked long...and the great charm of all power is modesty."
"I'm not afraid of storms...for I'm learning how to sail my ship."

*Dame Margot Asquith*
"The elements of greatness are...humbleness, freedom from self, intrepid courage, and the power to love."

*Aristotle*
"Wicked people obey from fear...good people, from love."

*Josh Billings*
"The best time for you to hold your tongue is...when you feel you must say something, or bust!"

*Napoleon Bonaparte*
"He who fears being conquered...is sure of defeat."
"Soldiers usually win the battles, and generals... get credit for them."

*Fannie Brice*
"Let the world know you as you are...not as you think you should be."

*Charles Buxton*
"You will never 'find time' for anything...if you want time, you must make it."

*Rachael Carson*
"The discipline of the writer is...to be still and listen to what her subject has to tell her."

*Miguel de Cervantes*
"Jests that give pain...are no jests!"

*Agatha Christie*
"It's astonishing in this world how things...don't turn out at all the way you expect them to!"

*Sir Winston Churchill*
"A fanatic is one who...can't change his mind and won't change the subject."
"Responsibility is...the price of greatness."

*Cicero*
"Man is his own...worst enemy."
"To the sick, where there is life...there is hope."

*Collette*
"In the face of boredom...I turn into a wretched and, if necessary, ferocious creature."

*Confucius*
"Study the past if you would...divine the future."
"When prosperity comes...do not use all of it."

*Charles de Gaulle*
"Silence is...the ultimate weapon of power."

*Joan Didion*
"I am what I am...to look for reasons is beside the point."

*Alexander Dumas*
"All for one...and one for all!"

*Baroness Marie Ebner von Eschenbach*
"We are so vain...that we even care for the opinion of those we don't care for!"

*Thomas Edison*
"Show me a thoroughly satisfied person...and I will show you a failure."

*Dwight D. Eisenhower*
"Leadership is the art of getting someone else to...do something you want done because *he* wants to do it."
"The future of this republic is in the hands of...the American voter."

*Ralph Waldo Emerson*
"What you do speaks so loudly...I cannot hear what you say."
"The only way to have a friend...is to be one."
"The reward of a thing well done is...to have done it."
"Concentration is...the secret of strength."

*Lord Essex*
"Genius is entitled to respect only when...it promotes the peace and improves the happiness of mankind."

*Susanne la Follette*
"Laws are felt only when...an individual comes into contact with them."
"Until economic freedom is attained for everybody...there can be no real freedom for anybody."

*Anne Frank*
"Parents can only give good advice or put children on the right paths...The final forming of a person's character lies in their own hands."

*Benjamin Franklin*
"Take time for all things...great haste makes waste."
"He that falls in love with himself...will have no rivals."
"A little neglect...may breed great mischief."
"A place for everything...everything in its place."

"Never leave that till tomorrow...which you can do today."
"Three may keep a secret...if two of them are dead!"
"There was never a good war...or a bad peace."

*Betty Friedan*
"That we have not made any respectable attempt to meet the special educational needs of women is the clearest possible evidence...that our educational objectives have been based on the vocational patterns of men."

*Robert Frost*
"Half the world is composed of people who have something to say and can't say it...and the other half who have nothing to say and keep on saying it."

*Galileo*
"You cannot teach a person anything...you can only help him to find it in himself."

*Mavis Gallant*
"Now that he was rich...he was not thought ignorant anymore; merely eccentric."

*Ellen Glasgow*
"The person who was not content to do small things well...would leave great things undone."

*Angelina Grimke*
"So precious a talent as intellect never was given...to be wrapt in a napkin and buried in the earth."

*Uta Hagen*
"We must overcome the notion that we must be regular...it robs you of the chance to be extraordinary and leads you to do the mediocre."

*Nathan Hale*
"I only regret that I have...but one life to give for my country."

*Don Herrold*
"The brighter you are...the more you have to learn."

*Thomas Jefferson*
"We hold these truths to be self-evident...that all men are created equal."
"Eternal vigilance is...the price of liberty."

*Helen Keller*
"One can never consent to creep...when one feels the impulse to soar!"

*John Fitzgerald Kennedy*
"Let us never negotiate out of fear...but let us never fear to negotiate."
"Ask not what your country can do for you...ask what you can do for your country."

"Those who make peaceful revolution impossible...will make violent revolution inevitable."

*Dr. Martin Luther King, Jr.*
"We must learn to live together as brothers...or perish as fools."

*General Robert E. Lee*
"It is well that war is so terrible...we shouldn't grow too fond of it."

*Sam Levenson*
"Insanity is hereditary...you can get it from your children!"

*Abraham Lincoln*
"The probability that we may fail in the struggle...ought not to deter us from the support of a cause we believe to be just."
"With malice toward none, with charity for all...let us finish the work we are in."
"You can fool some of the people all of the time, and all of the people some of the time, but...you cannot fool all of the people all of the time."
"As I would not be a slave...I would not be a master. This is my idea of democracy."
"A house divided against itself...cannot stand."

*Anne Morrow Lindbergh*
"It isn't for the moment you are struck that you need courage...but for the long uphill climb back to sanity and faith and security."

*Henry Wadsworth Longfellow*
"It takes less time to do a thing right...than it does to explain why you did it wrong."

*James Russell Lowell*
"The foolish and the dead alone...never change their minds."

*Margaret Mead*
"We're living beyond our means. We have developed a lifestyle...that is draining the earth of its priceless and irreplaceable resources."

*A.A. Milne*
"One of the advantages of being disorderly is that...one is constantly making exciting discoveries!"

*J.P. Morgan*
"A person always has two reasons for doing anything...a good reason and the real reason."

*Governeur Morris*
"United we stand...divided we fall."

*Anais Nin*
"What I cannot love, I overlook...Is that not real friendship?"
"When one is pretending...the entire body revolts."

*Thomas Paine*
"These are the times...that try men's souls."
"What we obtain too cheaply...we esteem too lightly."

*Reverend Dr. Norman Vincent Peale*
"Believe you are defeated, believe it long enough...and it is likely to become a fact."

*William Penn*
"He that does good for good's sake seeks...neither paradise nor reward, but is assured of both."

*Dorothy Miller Richardson*
"People want recognition of their work...to help them believe in themselves."

*Sylvia Rimm*
"The surest path to positive self-esteem is to be successful at something...one perceived would be difficult."

*Rodin*
"Nothing is a waste of time...if you use the experience wisely."

*Will Rogers*
"Everything is funny as long as...it's happening to someone else.
"Get someone else to blow your horn...and the sound will travel twice as far."

*Eleanor Roosevelt*
"No one can make you feel inferior...without your consent."
"It is not fair to ask of others...what you are not willing to do yourself."

*Franklin Delano Roosevelt*
"The only thing we have to fear...is fear itself."

*Theodore Roosevelt*
"The government is us...We are the government: you and I."

*George Santayana*
"Those who cannot remember the past...are condemned to repeat it."

*William Shakespeare*
"How sharper than a serpent's tooth is to have...a thankless child."
"What's in a name?  That which we call a rose by any other name...would smell as sweet."

*George Bernard Shaw*
"Youth is a wonderful thing...what a crime it is to waste it on children!"

*Socrates*
"False words are not only evil in themselves...but they infect the soul with evil."

*Gertrude Stein*
"Everyone gets so much information all day...that they lose their common sense."

*Jonathan Swift*
"There is none so blind...as those who will not see."
"Necessity is...the mother of invention."

*Alfred, Lord Tennyson*
"It is better to have loved and lost...than to have never loved at all."

*Henry David Thoreau*
"The mass of people lead lives of...quiet desperation."

*Harry S. Truman*
"The White House is...the finest prison in the world."
"The buck...stops here."
"If you can't stand the heat...get out of the kitchen."

*Mark Twain*
"Man is the only animal...that blushes—or needs to."
"Familiarity...breeds contempt."
"When I was a boy of 14, my father was so ignorant that I could hardly stand to have the old man around....But when I got to be 21, I was astonished at how much the old man had learned in seven years!"

*Abigail Van Buren*
"People who fight fire with fire...usually end up with ashes."

*Booker T. Washington*
"You can never hold a person down...without staying down with him."

*John Greenleaf Whittier*
"Of all sad words of tongue or pen, the saddest are these...what *might* have been."

*Virginia Woolf*
"The history of man's opposition to women's emancipation has been more interesting than...the story of the emancipation itself."
"If you do not tell the truth about yourself...you cannot tell it about other people."

# ALPHABET SOUP

*Directions:* Give students copies of the Alphabet Soup handout on page 148. Allow them to work on these puzzles for several days. Tell them that if there are any puzzles they simply *can't* solve, they may come to you for clues. Students who finish early may create their own puzzles to add to the list.*

*Clues and Answers:* Following are clues and answers to the puzzles, numbered to correspond with the student handout:

1. CLUE: A game.
   ANSWER: 20 Questions (Animal, Vegetable, or Mineral).

2. CLUE: A nursery rhyme.
   ANSWER: 10 Little Indians.

3. CLUE: A superstition.
   ANSWER: 7 years of bad luck for breaking a mirror.

4. CLUE: A measurement.
   ANSWER: 2000 pounds in a ton.

5. CLUE: A musical.
   ANSWER: 76 trombones that led the big parade.

6. CLUE: Communication.
   ANSWER: 10 digits in a telephone number (including the area code).

7. CLUE: Politics.
   ANSWER: 18 1/2 minutes erased from the Watergate tapes.

8. CLUE: History.
   ANSWER: 3 parts into which ancient Gaul was divided.

9. CLUE: Transportation.
   ANSWER: 5 tires on a car (including the spare in the trunk).

10. CLUE: A saying.
    ANSWER: 1 rotten apple in every barrel.

11. CLUE: A sport.
    ANSWER: 3 strikes, you're out at the old ball game.

12. CLUE: A game.
    ANSWER: 9 squares in Tic-Tac-Toe.

13. CLUE: A song or chant.
    ANSWER: 15 men on a dead man's chest.

14. CLUE: A fairy tale.
    ANSWER: 7 dwarves with Snow White.

15. CLUE: Government.
    ANSWER: 9 justices of the Supreme Court.

16. CLUE: A sport.
    ANSWER: 6 players on a polo team.

17. CLUE: Music.
    ANSWER: 4 strings on a violin or viola.

18. CLUE: A bad habit.
    ANSWER: 20 cigarettes in a package.

19. CLUE: Religions.
    ANSWER: 66 books of the Bible (in the King James Version).

20. CLUE: Music.
    ANSWER: 88 = piano keys.

# TRANSMOGRIFICATIONS

*Directions:* Students use dictionaries to translate sayings from complex to simple language. Later, they use a thesaurus to translate sayings from simple to complex language.

Students may add their own examples to those on the lists shown here. They do not share their answers until work is completed.

For more about transmogrifications, see Vocabulary Builders on page 98.

*For the primary grades:* Use first lines of nursery rhymes. Examples, with answers:

1. Scintillate, scintillate, asteroid minific. (Twinkle, twinkle, little star.)

2. Bleat, bleat, ebony ewe. (Baa, baa, black sheep.)

3. Petite lad cerulean, approach and huff your trumpet. (Little Boy Blue, come blow your horn.)

4. Croon a ditty of six coins. (Sing a song of sixpence.)

5. A petite swine traveled to the retail stores. (This little piggy went to market.)

---

*Other challenging puzzles and brain teasers gifted students enjoy appear monthly in *Games Magazine*. For information, call 1-800-950-6339.

# ALPHABET SOUP

**Directions:** Solve the following alphabet puzzles. You may take several days to work on them. If there are any you can't figure out, you may ask the teacher for clues.

**Example:** 20 = Q. (A.V. or M.)
Clue: A game
Solution: 20 = Questions (Animal, Vegetable, or Mineral)

**1.** 20 = Q. (A.V. or M.)

**2.** 10 = L.I.

**3.** 7 = Y. of B.L. for B. a M.

**4.** 2000 = P. in a T.

**5.** 76 = T. that L. the B.P.

**6.** 10 = D. in a T.N. (including the A.C.)

**7.** 18 1/2 = M.E. from the W.T.

**8.** 3 = P. into which A. G. was D.

**9.** 5 = T. on a C. (including the S. in the T.)

**10.** 1 = R.A. in E.B.

**11.** 3 = S.Y.O. at the O.B.G.

**12.** 9 = S. in T.T.T.

**13.** 15 = M. on a D.M.C.

**14.** 7 = D. with S.W.

**15.** 9 = J. of the S.C.

**16.** 6 = P. on a P.T.

**17.** 4 = S. on a V.

**18.** 20 = C. in a P.

**19.** 66 = B. of the B. (in the K.J.V.)

**20.** 88 = P.K.

6. John and Gillian ascended the mound. (Jack and Jill went up the hill.)

7. The capital of England's metal structure is collapsing. (London Bridge is falling down.)

8. John S. could ingest no gristle; his mate could ingest no gaunt. (Jack Spratt could eat no fat; his wife could eat no lean.)

9. Loop circularly the roseate, a cloth holder brimming with blossoms. (Ring around the rosy, a pocket full of posies.)

10. Sway-a-bye infant child, on the loftiest conifer. (Rock-a-bye baby, on the tree top.)

*For the upper grades:* Use sayings or adages. Examples, with answers:

1. Unpunctuality is preferable to failure to arrive. (Better late than never.)

2. An excess of forward motion results in careless squandering. (Haste makes waste.)

3. Consistent dedication to one's career-related pursuit without interludes of disportment establishes John as a doltish shaveling. (All work and no play make Jack a dull boy.)

4. Immaculateness is proximate to rectitude. (Cleanliness is next to godliness.)

5. Benevolent deeds commence in one's domicile. (Charity begins at home.)

6. The stylus is more potent than the bayonet. (The pen is mightier than the sword.)

7. Male cadavers are incapable of relating any testimony. (Dead men tell no tales.)

8. Neophytes' serendipity. (Beginner's luck.)

9. The vegetation appears to have a deeper hue when situated across a stile. (The grass is always greener on the other side of the fence.)

10. A pair of skulls is more valuable than half of two. (Two heads are better than one.)

# SILLY NILLIES

*Directions:* Students make up two-word definitions for phrases provided. The words must 1) rhyme and 2) have the same number of syllables. Students may add their own examples to those on the list shown on page 150.

*Answers:* Following are some possible definitions for the phrases listed, numbered to correspond with the student handout.

Don't give out any answers until the exercise is completed. Be sure to allow for other answers students can justify.

1. better sweater
2. wild child
3. wrong song
4. wee key
5. fat cat
6. sassy lassie
7. sky pie
8. flower power
9. thinner dinner
10. funny money
11. flower power
12. rational national
13. faster plaster
14. precise device
15. fission mission
16. scare pair
17. fight knight
18. pop top
19. hobby lobby
20. long songs

# SILLY NILLIES

**Directions:** Make up two-word definitions for these phrases. The words must 1) rhyme and 2) have the same number of syllables. You may create your own examples to add to the list.

**Examples:**
An escaped gander is a...loose goose.
I think Snickers' bars are...dandy candy.
A badly mixed-up newscast is...confusion diffusion.

1. An improved wool pullover is a... _____

2. An undisciplined youngster is a... _____

3. An out-of-tune chorus sings a... _____

4. A minuscule tool for unlocking things is a... _____

5. An overweight feline is a... _____

6. A girl who talks back to her parents is a... _____

7. Pizza served on the airplane is... _____

8. Group accomplishments from "hippies" of the 1960's were... _____

9. A meal for someone who is on a serious diet is a... _____

10. Coinage used to purchase items that cannot be bought with regular currency is... _____

11. A tall, strong rose on a very thick stem has... _____

12. A citizen who thinks very clearly on politics is... _____

13. A worker who puts walls into place speedily can do... _____

14. An instrument that is used for only one specialized task is a... _____

15. Someone who wants to get an okay to build an atomic device is on a... _____

16. Two very ugly monsters make a... _____

17. A brave soldier on a white horse who saves a town from a dragon is a... _____

18. A jar lid that comes off with very little effort is a... _____

19. A display of people's handiwork in the registration area of a hotel is a... _____

20. An opera contains a series of... _____

# SOURCES FOR GIFTED EDUCATION MATERIALS

A.W. Peller
Bright Ideas for the Gifted and Talented Catalog
210 Sixth Avenue
PO Box 106
Hawthorne, NJ 07507
Toll-free telephone: 1-800-451-7450
*A distributor for many other companies.*

The Albert Ellis Institute
45 E. 65th Street
New York, NY 10021
Toll-free telephone: 1-800-323-4738
*Formerly the Institute for Rational Emotive Therapy. Materials to help chidren and adults choose rational behaviors in order to feel more in control of their lives.*

Apple Publishing
W. 6050 Apple Road
Watertown, WI 53094
Toll-free telephone: 1-800-475-1118
*Sylvia Rimm's materials on underachievement.*

Center for Creative Learning
4152 Independence Court, Suite C-7
Sarasota, FL 34234-2147
Telephone: (941) 351-8862
*Donald Treffinger and colleagues help teachers learn about and use Creative Problem Solving in the classroom.*

Challenge Magazine: Reaching and
Teaching the Gifted Child
May be ordered through:
Good Apple
Box 55681
Boulder, CO 80322
Telephone: 1-800-264-9873
*Ready-to-photocopy enrichment activities for gifted kids.*

Creative Learning Press
1733 Storrs Road
Holiday Mall
Storrs, CT 06268
Telephone: (860) 429-8118
*Publisher of Renzulli materials, materials from the National Research Center for Gifted Education, and unique resources for helping kids do high quality independent projects.*

Creative Publications
5040 W. 111 Street
Oaklawn, IL 60453
Toll-free telephone: 1-800-624-0822
In Illinois: 1-800-435-5843
*Problem-solving materials in all subject areas.*

Critical Thinking Books and Software Press
PO Box 448
Pacific Grove, CA 93950
Toll-free telephone: 1-800-458-4849
*Formerly Midwest Publications, this company offers materials that provide students with great activities for challenging their thinking abilities.*

The Curriculum Project
3300 Bee Cane Road, Suite 650-141
Austin, TX 78746
Telephone: (512) 263-3089
*Product guides by John Samara that serve as assessment tools for gifted students' independent studies.*

Dale Seymour Catalogs
PO Box 10888
Palo Alto, CA 94303
Toll-free telephone: 1-800-872-1100
*Math and English resources.*

Dandy Lion
3563 Sueldo, Suite L
San Luis Obispo, CA 93401
Toll-free telephone: 1-800-776-8032
*Lots of challenging activity books with an emphasis
on challenging children in the primary grades.*

Educational Teaching Aids
620 Lakeview Parkway
Vernon Hills, IL 60061
Toll-free telephone: 1-800-445-5985
*Source of Versa-Tiles, etc.*

Engine-Uity, Ltd.
PO Box 9610
Phoenix, AZ 85068
Telephone: (602) 997-7144
*Packets for learning centers using Bloom's Taxonomy.*

Free Spirit Publishing Inc.
400 First Avenue North, Suite 616
Minneapolis, MN 55401
Toll-free telephone: 1-800-735-7323
*Learning and lifeskills materials for children and teens,
teachers and parents; special emphasis on gifted.
Request a free catalog.*

Future Problem Solving
2500 Packard Road, Suite 110
Ann Arbor, MI 48104
Telephone: (313) 973-8781
*Center for information and materials about the national
Future Problem Solving competition.*

Gifted, Creative, and Talented Magazine
PO Box 6448
Mobile, AL 36660
Toll-free telephone: 1-800-476-8711
*Current issues and practices in gifted education.*

Gifted Psychology Press
Box 5057
Scottsdale, AZ 85261
Telephone: (602) 368-7862
*Dr. James Webb and others present materials to help
understand gifted students' social/emotional needs.*

Greenhaven Press
PO Box 289009
San Diego, CA 92128-9009
Telephone: (619) 485-7424
*Debate material, especially the "Opposing Viewpoints"
series of books.*

The Institute for Rational Emotive Therapy
*See* The Albert Ellis Institute

Interact
PO Box 997-H91
Lakeside, CA 92040
Toll-free telephone: 1-800-359-0961
*Simulations.*

Learning Styles Network
St. John's University
Grand Central and Utopia Parkways
Jamaica, NY 11439
Telephone: (718) 990-6335
*Ask for a resource brochure with information on CAPs
(Contract Activity Packages).*

Learning to Learn Company
895 Bellewood Drive SE
Kentwood, MI 49508
Telephone: (616) 249-3983
*Merit projects, designed by Phil Schlemmer, provide challenging
independent study units for middle school students.*

News Currents
PO Box 52
Madison, WI 53701
Toll-free telephone: 1-800-356-2303, ext. 2
*Weekly current events filmstrip with teacher guide; for
grades 3 and up.*

Ohio Psychology Press
*See* Gifted Psychology Press

Philosophy for Children
IAPC Montclair State College
Upper Montclair, NJ 07043
Telephone: (973) 655-4277
*Teaching materials designed to introduce philosophy to
students of all ages.*

Pieces of Learning
PO Box 340667
Dayton, OH 45434-0067
Toll-free telephone: 1-800-729-5137
*Wide variety of activity and information books on teaching
for thinking and gifted education.*

Prufrock Press
PO Box 8813
Waco, TX 76714
Toll-free telephone: 1-800-998-2208
*Source for materials and resources for gifted high school
students. Also publishes the* Journal of Secondary
Gifted Education.

Thinking Caps Inc.
PO Box 26239
Phoenix, AZ 85068
Telephone: (602) 870-1527
Toll-free telephone: 1-800-529-5581
*Learning stations based on Bloom's Taxonomy.*

Zephyr Press
PO Box 66006-OL
Tucson, AZ 85728-6006
Toll-free telephone: 1-800-232-2187
www.zephyrpress.com
*Self-directed learning packets.*

# BIBLIOGRAPHY

Adderholdt-Elliott, Miriam. *Perfectionism: What's Bad about Being Too Good?* Minneapolis, MN: Free Spirit Publishing Inc., 1987.

Allen, Susan D. "Ability-Grouping Research Reviews: What Do They Say about Grouping and the Gifted?" *Educational Leadership* 48:6 (March, 1991): 60-65.

Bloom, Benjamin, *et al. Taxonomy of Educational Objectives: Handbook of the Cognitive Domain.* New York: Longman, 1984.

Brody, Linda, Susan Assouline, and Julian Stanley. "Five Years of Early Entrants: Predicting Successful Achievement in College." *Gifted Child Quarterly* 34:4 (Fall 1990): 138-142.

Chuska, Kenneth. *Gifted Learners K-12: A Practical Guide to Effective Curriculum and Teaching.* Bloomington, IN: National Educational Service, 1989.

Daniels, Paul. *Teaching the Gifted/Learning Disabled Child.* Rockville, MD: Aspen Publishing Company, 1983.

Eberle, Bob, and Bob Standish. *CPS (Creative Problem Solving) for Kids.* East Aurora, NY: D.O.K. Publishers, 1980.

Ellis, Albert. *How to Raise an Emotionally Happy, Healthy Child.* Hollywood, CA: Wilshire Books, 1966.
— and Robert Harper. *A New Guide to Rational Living.* Hollywood, CA: Wilshire Books, 1975.

Faelton, Sharon. *Tension Turnaround.* Emmaus, PA: Rodale Press, 1990.

Feldhusen, Hazel. *Individualized Teaching of Gifted Children in Regular Classrooms.* East Aurora, N.Y.: D.O.K. Publishers, 1986.

Feldhusen, John. "Synthesis of Research on Gifted Youth." *Educational Leadership* 46:6 (March, 1989): 6-11.
— Theron Proctor, and Kathryn Black. "Guidelines for Early Entrance into Kindergarten" (1988). Write to: Gifted Education Resource Institute, Purdue University, South Campus Court—W, West Lafayette, IN 47907.

Galbraith, Judy. *The Gifted Kids Survival Guide (For Ages 10 & Under).* Minneapolis, MN: Free Spirit Publishing Inc., 1984.

Galbraith, Judy, and James Delisle. *The Gifted Kids Survival Guide: A Teen Handbook,* Revised and Updated Edition. Minneapolis, MN: Free Spirit Publishing Inc., 1996.

Grun, Bernard. *Timetables of History: Horizontal Linkage of People and Events.* New Third Revised Edition. New York: Touchstone Books, 1991.

Halsted, Judith W. *Guiding Gifted Readers.* Columbus, OH: Ohio Psychology Publishing Co., 1988.

Hauser, Paula, and Gayle Nelson. *Books for the Gifted Child.* New York: R.R. Bowker Co., 1988.

Heacox, Diane. *Up from Underachievement: How Teachers, Students, and Parents Can Work Together to Promote Student Success.* Minneapolis, MN: Free Spirit Publishing Inc., 1991.

Hegeman, Kathryn. *Gifted Children in the Regular Classroom.* Monroe, NY: Trillium Press, 1987.

Johnson, David, and Roger Johnson. "What to Say to Parents of Gifted Students." *The Cooperative Link* 5:2, 1-3. 152 Write to: Cooperative Learning Center, 150 Pillsbury Drive, Minneapolis, MN 55455, or call (612) 624-7031.

Juntune, Joyce. *Creative Problem Solving for the Classroom Teacher.* San Ramon, CA: One Hundred Twenty Creations, 1982.

Kerr, Barbara. *Smart Girls, Gifted Women.* Columbus, OH: Ohio Psychology Publishing Co., 1986.

Knaus, William. *Rational Emotive Education: A Manual for Elementary School Teachers.* New York: Institute for Rational Living, 1974.

Kulik, James, and Chen-Lin Kulik. "Ability Grouping and Gifted Students." In Nicolas Colangelo and Gary Davis, eds., *Handbook of Gifted Education.* Needham Heights, MA: Allyn and Bacon, 1991.
— "Synthesis of Research on Effects of Accelerated Instruction." *Educational Leadership* 42:2 (October, 1984): 84-89.

Mills, Carol, and William Durden. "Finding an Optimal Match: A Reasonable Response to the Use of Cooperative Learning, Ability Grouping, and Tracking." *Gifted Child Quarterly* 36:1 (Winter 1992): 11-16.

Morris, William, and Mary Morris. *Dictionary of Word and Phrase Origins.* New York: Harper and Row, 1971.

Parke, Beverly. *Gifted Students in Regular Classrooms.* Boston: Allyn and Bacon, 1989.

Renzulli, Joseph. *The Enrichment Triad Model.* Mansfield Center, CT: Creative Learning Press, 1977.
— ed. *Systems and Models for Developing Programs for the Gifted and Talented.* Mansfield Center, CT: Creative Learning Press, 1986.
— "The Multiple Menu Model for Developing Differentiated Curriculum for the Gifted and Talented." *Gifted Child Quarterly* 32:3 (Fall 1988): 298-306.
— and Sally Reis. *The Schoolwide Enrichment Model.* Mansfield Center, CT: Creative Learning Press, 1985.

Rimm, Sylvia. *Underachievement Syndrome: Causes and Cures.* Watertown, WI: Apple Publishing Co., 1986.
— *How to Parent So Children Will Learn.* Watertown, WI: Apple Publishing Co., 1989.

Robinson, Ann. "Cooperation or Exploitation: The Argument against Cooperative Learning for Talented Students." *Journal for the Education of the Gifted* 14:1 (Fall 1990): 9-27.

Rogers, Karen. *The Relationship of Grouping Practices to the Education of the Gifted and Talented Learner: Research-Based Decision Making* (1991). Write to: National Research Center on the Gifted and Talented, Storrs, CT 06268.

Schmitz, Connie, and Judy Galbraith. *Managing the Social and Emotional Needs of the Gifted: A Teacher's Survival Guide.* Minneapolis, MN: Free Spirit Publishing Inc., 1985.

Schunk, Dale. "Peer Models and Children's Behavioral Change." *Review of Educational Research* 57:2 (Summer 1987): 149-174.

Sengal, Daniel. "The Other Crisis in Our Schools: Our Brightest Students Are Getting a 'Dumbed-Down' Education." *Reader's Digest* (April, 1992): 111-115.

Shanahan, Timothy, ed. *Reading and Writing Together: New Perspectives for the Classroom.* Norwood, MA: Christopher Gordon Publishers, Inc., 1990.

Sicola, P. "Where Do Gifted Students Fit: An Examination of Middle School Philosophy As It Relates to Ability Grouping and the Gifted Learner." *Journal for the Education of the Gifted* 14:1 (Fall 1990): 37-49.

Silverman, Linda. "Instructional Strategies for the Gifted." In E.L. Meyers and T.M. Skrtic, eds., *Exceptional Children and Youth.* Third Edition. Denver, CO: Love Publishing, 1988.

Slavin, Robert. "Ability Grouping, Cooperative Learning, and the Gifted." *Journal for the Education of the Gifted* 14:1 (Fall 1990): 3-8.

Smutney, Joan Franklin, Kathleen Veenker, and Stephen Veenker. *Your Gifted Child: How to Recognize and Develop the Special Talents in Your Child from Birth to Age Seven.* New York: Facts on File, 1989.

Starko, Alane. *It's About Time.* Mansfield Center, CT: Creative Learning Press, 1986.

Stewig, Johan, and Sam Sebesta, eds. *Using Literature in the Elementary Classroom.* Urbana, IL: National Council of Teachers of English, 1989.

Taylor, Roger. *Reshaping the Curriculum: Integrate, Differentiate, Compact, and Think.* Oakbrook, IL: Curriculum Design for Excellence, 1991.

Tierney, Robert, Mark Carter, and Laura Desai. *Portfolio Assessment in the Reading-Writing Classroom.* Norwood, MA: Christopher Gordon Publishers, Inc., 1991.

Treffinger, Donald, Robert Hohn, and John Feldhusen. *Reach Each You Teach.* East Aurora, NY: D.O.K. Publishers, 1979.

Winebrenner, Susan. *Super Sentences.* Mansfield Center, CT: Creative Learning Press, 1989.
— and Barbara Devlin. "Cluster Grouping Fact Sheet: How to Provide Full-Time Services for Gifted Students on Existing Budgets" (1991). Write to: Phantom Press, 15 Lombard Circle, Lombard, IL 60148.

Wlodkowski, Raymond. *Motivation and Teaching: A Practical Guide.* Washington, DC: National Education Association, 1986.

Wolfe, Jane, and Michael French. *Surviving Gifted Attention Deficit Disorder Children in the Classroom* (1991). Bowling Green, OH: Bowling Green State University.

Zarnowski, Myra. *Learning about Biographies.* Urbana, IL: National Council of Teachers of English, 1990.

# INDEX

## ABOUT THE AUTHOR

Susan Winebrenner has a Master's Degree in Curriculum and Instruction and a Bachelor's Degree in Education. She was a gifted program coordinator, teacher of gifted students, and classroom teacher for 20 years before becoming a full-time consultant in staff development. Today she presents workshops across the United States on a variety of topics, but her first love is still teaching gifted kids.

Susan's outside-of-work passions include sailing, singing, and learning how to improvise on the piano. Presently, she lives in Brooklyn, Michigan.

Susan would be happy to talk to people in your district about presenting workshops for your staff. Her topics include:

- "Teaching Gifted Kids in the Regular Classroom,"

- "Teaching Kids with Learning Difficulties in the Regular Classroom,"

- "Teaching Successfully in the Mixed-Ability Classroom,"and

- "Providing Enriched Learning Activities for All Students."

*Please contact Susan Winebrenner c/o Free Spirit Publishing Inc.,*
*400 First Avenue North, Suite 616,*
*Minneapolis, MN 55401*
*telephone (612) 338-2068*
*or email* help4kids@freespirit.com

# Other Great Books from Free Spirit

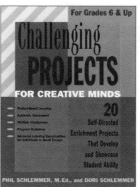